Not J...

CARWYN JONES is best known for his prominent role in British politics as the First Minister of Wales from 2009 until 2018. Born in Morriston to a Welsh-speaking family, he grew up in Bridgend, and worked as a barrister before his political career. He is married with two children and lives in Bridgend.

ALUN GIBBARD is a full-time author from Llanelli who has published many non-fiction books, and one novel. He also contributes to the weekly magazine *Golwg*. He was a broadcaster for a quarter of a century before starting his writing career, and still participates in radio and TV programmes.

CARWYN JONES

With Alun Gibbard

NOT JUST POLITICS

HEADLINE PUBLISHING GROUP
An Hachette UK Company

ACCENT

I Lisa.
Go raibh maith agat.

First published in 2020 by Headline Accent
An imprint of HEADLINE PUBLISHING GROUP

First published in paperback in 2021 by Headline Accent
An imprint of HEADLINE PUBLISHING GROUP

1

Cataloguing in Publication Data is available from the British Library

Paperback ISBN 978 1 4722 7203 4

Designed and typeset by EM&EN
Printed and bound in Great Britain by Clays Ltd, Elcograf S.p.A.

Head   le
pro   r
con   WEST NORTHAMPTONSHIRE   d
to   COUNCIL

       80003738829

       Askews & Holts

       BT

www.hachette.co.uk

Acknowledgements

Lisa, for being there and for her love and forebearance.

Seren and Ruairi, for all the times when I wasn't around but for being there for me.

My mother and father, for giving me everything parents could.

Alun Gibbard, for his patience and experience in writing this book.

Headline Accent, for having the faith to publish this book.

Leigh-Ann Regan, whose idea this was.

The National Assembly Labour Party, for their unfailing support for nine years.

Rose Stewart and my Private Office, for keeping me (and Wales) on track.

Chris, Clare and Lauren, for being a superb constituency team.

Jo, Matt, Huw, Jane and Simon for all the advice and support over the years and for being a wonderful group of people.

The Aber Boys, for thirty years of friendship.

The 'Coven' and spouses for their support.

The Murray family for making me one of their own.

And last, but not least, the Bridgend Constituency Labour Party and the people of Bridgend for their support over five elections.

Contents

ONE

Finding the Coalface

It was a time of political activism not seen for decades in the United Kingdom: a monumental, aggressive and often violent clash of diametrically opposed ideologies, with a great deal of passionate emotion, based on generations of proud heritage, thrown into the mix. The 1984 Miners' Strike was history in the making. A Conservative Government relentlessly pursued a policy to close as many coal mines as possible. Prime Minister Margaret Thatcher believed that there were too many mines that weren't running efficiently and that this was hampering the growth of the UK economy generally.

The miners of Wales, Scotland and England, on the other hand, saw things differently. They disagreed with the Tory interpretation of the economics in most cases, saying that a broader political agenda was colouring the Government's view of the facts and figures. But also, for them, mining was so much more than just economics.

It was, fundamentally, a way of life. If it wasn't for coal in areas such as South Wales, Yorkshire and the North-East of England, whole villages and communities would not have existed. So it wasn't all about the wage packet. It was about the birth certificate too. It was the geography of identity, the psycho-geography of who a people are. In my own region, 'the Valleys', as they are typically referred to, are valleys of coal – from the Ebbw in the east to the Gwendraeth in the west. As coal seams were discovered and pits were sunk, people poured in, houses were built and streets were formed. Quite often those streets appeared so quickly that there was no time to name them before moving on to build the next new street.

No wonder, then, that the miners fought tooth and nail to oppose the Government's plans. For them, that fight resulted in a strike which would last an entire year. Well over a hundred thousand miners refused to work, and, as a result, they were without pay for the full twelve months. There were ugly picket-line clashes, loss of life, and family feuds that tore at the fabric of British life in so many areas. The recriminations can still be felt today in both families and communities across the South Wales I was brought up in.

In my own locality, while the '84 strike was on, there was a story of a miners' library that still refused membership to family members of a miner who had broken another coal strike in the early 1900s. In '84, family members who were out on strike would not speak to other family members who had decided to break the strike and return to work. Such workers were given the epithet 'scabs', and quite often photographs of them would be put on posters placed in public places in order to name and shame them. It's not only the seams that run deep in coal mining communities.

Of the thirteen individual coalfields in England, Scotland and Wales, the most united support for the strike once it had started was in South Wales, with 99.6% of the 21,500 National Union of Mineworkers members in the area still supporting the strike after six months. That figure only dropped to 93% after a year out on strike.

It was impossible to ignore the Miners' Strike in the South Wales of my upbringing. It was there at breakfast time in print and at supper time on TV. People talked about it in school, on the streets and at home. 'Victory to the miners' slogans were painted on the side of bridges, posters asking for food for mining families were put on lamp posts, village halls put on fund-raising events, and miners organized fund-raising tours to other communities outside the coalfields, such as Brixton in London. All this and more was happening as the union officials negotiated and protested. At coal mine and steelwork picket lines, confrontations between miners and police led to over 10,000 arrests and five deaths.

Meanwhile, I was not exactly at the heart of the primary industrial conflict that the nations of the UK had seen for decades. As the strike got redder and redder in tooth and claw, I had just started my first Saturday job in Tesco. But, for seventeen-year-old me, having a weekend job and earning my first ever wage was a big step. I was a million miles away from the dust of heavy industry, and not just because my own particular coalface was endless rows of trolleys. I was in Bridgend, which wasn't even in the South Wales coalfield. There were no mines there. There were some in neighbouring villages and valleys, such as the Garw, the Llynfi and Ogmore. But none in Bridgend. Never had been.

But there was no such thing as a non-coal mining area in the South Wales of the 1980s, especially during the strike. The statistics mentioned earlier give some considerable testimony to that. There might not have been any actual mines in Bridgend, but there was no hiding from the mining heritage and culture that the pits engendered. That's exactly what hit me quite forcefully on many a Saturday in Tesco.

While going about my work, there was a regular occurrence that left an increasing impression on me. As miners and their supporters came to Bridgend town to collect money to support the striking cause, they would bring their collection cans to Tesco. There I would see shoppers put five- and ten-pound notes in the boxes. Not just occasionally, but regularly. The ten-pound contributions were more than I would earn for a full day's work. I was amazed that people could give so much money to support the miners in a town where there weren't any mines. These people, I thought, must really believe in what the miners are doing. There's no doubt that many living in Bridgend would have had family connections with miners in other areas, and many came into town from mining areas. But, still, that was not true of them all, not by far. What was it that made people who didn't work underground want to part with such large amounts of money in order to support those who did? This was a question that went round and round in my head for months.

Individual incidents from the strike itself started to sear themselves into my mind. One in particular made me ask new questions. A taxi driver was killed while taking a miner who had chosen to break the strike to his pit. Some striking miners, in their efforts to show their displeasure with that miner's decision to return, wanted to frighten him away. They threw concrete slabs from a footbridge into the path of the taxi on the road below. The intention was to make the miner think again about returning to work and to make the taxi driver think twice about taking him there. But the slabs smashed through the windscreen of the taxi, killing the driver, David Wilkie. An industrial conflict that had seen plenty of picket-line violence now had a death to deal with.

That fact alone made an impression on me, as it did on everyone else. Loss of life is a serious consequence of an industrial conflict. Understandably, it escalated the situation significantly, as all sides tried to respond appropriately to the tragedy while still maintaining their original stand on the conflict itself. But what added to the emotional impact for me was where that miner was going. He was on his way to Merthyr Vale Colliery. Overlooking that pit was the village of Aberfan. Less than twenty years before the strike and Wilkie's death, 116 children from that village had been killed when a coal tip slid down the side of the mountain, engulfing buildings on its way, including the school where the children were. Twenty-eight adults also lost their lives.

Some of the miners picketing in Merthyr Vale would have been involved in, or at least affected by, the Aberfan disaster. Some would have lost family members, others would have been on their hands and knees in the rubble, trying desperately to rescue any children, or to bring those killed out of what remained of the school. In 1984 they were on strike, fighting government attempts to close the industry that had made South Wales what it was, that had shaped communities such as Merthyr Vale and Aberfan. The injustice of the whole situation made a lasting impression on me.

My instant response was to feel the need to join a political party and get involved with the process, so as to deal with the strong sense of injustice I was feeling. But I wasn't sure which party I should become a member of – although there was no way in the world that it would be the Conservative Party. I didn't think that the Liberals appeared to offer much either. So I was down to either Plaid Cymru or the Labour Party. I took a while to think through what both parties stood for.

The epiphany eventually came in an unexpected place. I was in Court Colman Hotel near Bridgend, at yet another in a long chain of eighteenth birthday parties, thinking a great deal about where this political awakening should be channelled. It became evident that a political awakening was taking its own time to emerge in my mind, developing as and when it wanted to, and arriving at an answer when I least expected it. I was standing in the doorway of the hotel, talking to one of the girls at the party, when it struck. In mid conversation I turned to her and said, 'I'm going to join the Labour Party!' I doubt very much it was the chat-up line she was expecting. She certainly wasn't sure how to respond. But that was it. I had made my decision, in the last few weeks of the Miners' Strike, that I should nail my new-found political colours to the Labour Party's mast.

A few months later, I registered as a Labour Party member. That happened during my first few weeks at Aberystwyth University, in the September after the strike ended. My signature on that piece of paper was the culmination of almost a year's awakening, contemplation, deliberation and decision. It was the beginning of a conviction that still drives me and is central to who I am.

Many years later, when the film *Billy Elliot* came out, one scene in particular took me right back to the emotional impact of the strike on my eighteen-year-old self. It brought that era back to me. The sacrifices, the pride in the face of adversity, and the fraying bonds of solidarity as the strike went on. The film tells the story of the ballet-loving son of a Sheffield coalminer during that year-long strike. The tension of a young boy wanting to dance while his coalminer father is out on strike is a dramatic narrative. In one scene, the father has to break up the family's piano in order to have some firewood to heat the family home. That one act shows the way the strike affected families; they had to go without the basics of food and heat, which regularly pitted one family member up against another, causing tension and confrontation. It shows the coalminer's angst in his own home.

By the time the film appeared, I was at the end of my first year of being an Assembly Member in the newly constituted Senedd in Cardiff Bay. It was a different Wales to the one that saw my own personal political awakening. Wales now had an elected assembly to administer its own affairs. We had finally taken the first step on the devolution journey, after decades of debate and campaigning. But the needs we faced had their roots in the conflict of the mid-80s. In a few years, after the end of the strike, the coal mines had all gone and over 20,000 men who had worked in them now worked somewhere else, or didn't work at all. We were in the first decade of a Wales with no coal, bringing to an end over a century and a half of the central, formative relationship Wales had had with the black diamond. What drove me into politics was the determination that whole communities of workers up and down the UK should never be treated that way again. Margaret Thatcher brought me into politics, but not in the way she would have wanted.

My own family, my ancestors, had played their part in that relationship between the community and coal for many generations. So as the millennium drew to a close, I was seeing the end of a central pillar of my own family heritage, while at the same time beginning work in a brand-new institution that was to shape the new Wales necessitated by the demise of coal.

TWO

Three Village Roots

THE SMALL Carmarthenshire village of Brynaman has an influence and a significance way above its size. It lies where Carmarthenshire meets Neath Port Talbot. The river Aman divides the village into upper and lower – Upper being in Carmarthenshire and Lower in Neath Port Talbot. How many rugby teams in the UK have their changing rooms in one county but play in another? Brynaman RFC does.

For centuries Brynaman enjoyed a quiet rural and agricultural way of life. There was no need for clocks and watches. Things would happen when the seasons said they should. The people there, in the scattered farms and cottages, made their own world.

The discovery of coal and the coming of the railway in the century before last changed both the size of the village and its name. Up until the first trains steamed in, the settlement on that patch of land was known as

Gwter Fawr. It's referred to as such in the book *Wild Wales*, by Victorian traveller and writer George Borrow. That original name is the wonderful literal translation of 'Big Gutter'. Maybe the need for a name change is understandable? It must be said, however, that it does sound a lot worse in English than it does in Welsh. The new name, Brynaman, came from Brynaman House, the home of the man responsible for bringing the railway to the area. It says a great deal about the character of the village that, even with the boom of incoming industrialization, the place name wasn't anglicized.

Brynaman now had coal and steam trains to contend with, and this brought a lot more people to that quiet corner of the world. Coal gave them a reason to go there; the railway made it happen. It became a highly populated and thriving village. New streets appeared with startling regularity as the new workers needed new homes. But despite all this coming and going over many decades, the village remained predominantly Welsh-speaking, as the majority of those who came to work the new-found seams were originally from other parts of Wales. Consequently, a robust Welsh-language culture developed and prospered, and it had two homes: the chapel and the pub, both of which gave the community so much more than God and beer, respectively. Their social and cultural influence was all-pervasive.

Welsh chapels were home to a variety of events – religious and social – most days of the week. That's where the cultural celebration known as the Eisteddfod flourished, as adults and children alike competed against each other in verse and song, prose and poetry. The rugby club mentioned earlier gave the village an additional focus to what the pubs offered. It was eighty minutes of aggression on a pitch. It was also where men who faced the dangers of life underground could be together to wash away the dust and stress with a good pint of bitter.

It all sounds a bit romanticized now, and it's easy to think that nostalgia is influencing the recollection. But that is how it was. And, to a large extent, that's how it still is.

The same was true of two other villages that nestled around Brynaman – Cwmgors and Gwaun Cae Gurwen. The latter in more recent years is famous for producing two renowned giants in their particular fields. One is the international star of stage and screen Siân Phillips – it wasn't uncommon to see her and her then husband, Peter O'Toole, going for a pint in the pub on the square in Gwaun Cae Gurwen on their visits back to see family. The other was one of the best rugby players the world has ever seen, Gareth Edwards. Hundreds of people lined the streets of Y Waun (The Heath) when Gareth returned from the triumphant British Lions tour

of New Zealand in 1971. He was a central figure in the
Lions winning their first-ever test series victory in New
Zealand. The street party in his honour would certainly
have challenged any Coronation event!

THE THREE villages shared four collieries: The Mardy,
The East, Steer, and Cwmgors. Technically, however,
with a decidedly Welsh parochial allegiance, three of
those pits were in another village, Tairgwaith. That name
is only a few degrees away from Big Gutter in its pro-
saic qualities; it means 'the houses of the works', which
is right up there with Nowa Huta, near Kraków, which
means 'new factory'. Tairgwaith is very much regarded
as the unusual relative of the other three villages. When
The Mardy, The East and Steer were sunk, first of all,
that work was carried out by Irish workers. The locals
were happy to work there, but not happy to do the dirty
work of sinking the pit in the first place. When the Irish
came to do that, they lived in Tairgwaith. This set up an
'us and them' mentality in an area that was already very
small. That split in society even showed itself in the way
that the Welsh speakers from Brynaman, Cwmgors and
Gwaun Cae Gurwen reacted to the Welsh speakers in
Tairgwaith. If ever there was a discussion as to whether
someone could speak Welsh or not, and there was some
doubt about it, the reply would be, 'Yes, they do, but it's

Tairgwaith Welsh.' The not-so-subtle implication being that that village's Welsh wasn't as naturally 'Welsh' as in the big three. Needless to say, the people of Tairgwaith would see it very differently.

Those three villages grew to have their own strong, clear identities within the already separate identity of the West Wales coalfield. That broader West Walian separateness was initially formulated by the nature of the actual coal they were mining. It wasn't the steam coal or the house coal that the rest of the South Wales coalfield produced. This was the 'glo caled', the hard coal, the anthracite that was reputedly the best of its kind in the world. Added to the chemical nature of the coal itself was the existing cultural heritage of the area where it was found. This carboniferous collision, as artist Osi Rhys Osmond called it, created a robust and distinctive community. The three villages at the top end of the Aman Valley developed an identity within that identity, their own version of anthracite culture.

Keeping a watchful eye on all three villages is the Black Mountain, one of the wildest places in Wales. It gives the area its remoteness and its ruggedness. It is also a dramatic backdrop to the folklore that has passed down from generation to generation. Myth and fable fall with the mountain breeze over the people of Brynaman, Cwmgors and Gwaun Cae Gurwen. The stories of the

Lady of the Lake and the Wild Boar from the medieval collection of Welsh tales, the *Mabinogi*, the oldest collection of prose in British literature, have informed the culture of its people for centuries as they cared for the soil that was in their blood. Coal and steam did not displace them.

Among the crowds who flocked to this part of the coalfield within a coalfield were my great-grandparents. They went there because coal called them. Subsequently, my family, since the time of Victoria, was shaped by this particular, very local manifestation of industry and culture. Their migration was instigated in search of work. They came from many different communities, but all were rooted in West Wales. My gene pool is very, very small. I often wonder how I turned out the way I have, as I am by far the tallest in my family, going back a long while. My two grandfathers were about 5'6"/5'7".

MY GREAT-GRANDFATHER, John David Howells, was the eldest of thirteen children from the village of Gwynfe, on the other side of the Black Mountain. He was a carpenter who heard that there were coal mines opening in the area, so he decided to walk over the mountain to look for new work – and found it as a carpenter, an undertaker and a builder. He married Catherine Hugh, from Aberdare. My other maternal great-grandparents were

David and Jane Lloyd, he from Aberaeron, she from Brynaman. David worked underground as a haulier. On my father's side, his father's parents were James Jones, a shopkeeper originally from St Clears near Carmarthen, and Elizabeth from Brynaman. Completing the picture, his mother, Katy Hopkin, was the daughter of Will and Rachie Hopkin. He was a collier and they lived in Gwaun Cae Gurwen.

As happens so often in learning about your family history, you uncover some things that are a bit of a surprise. When my great-uncle died, we discovered that his parents, my Lloyd great-grandparents, were married in September 1912, just three months before he was born. Back then, in the community they were in, having a baby out of wedlock would have been nothing short of a scandal. The fact we didn't find that out as a family until after my great-uncle's death shows how deep that family secret had been buried for decades.

They had all died before I was born, bar one: Jane Lloyd. She lived for six weeks after I was born and I have photos of her holding me in her arms. It's a sign of how hard life was then that she was seventy-eight when she died but looked a lot older.

My two grandfathers came from Brynaman, with one grandmother from Cwmgors and the other from Gwaun Cae Gurwen. I only knew one of my grandmothers, as the other died of cancer in 1958. My maternal grand-father, Leslie Howells, was known as Les JD, because his dad, John David, was an undertaker, carrying on from what his father did. For some reason, I called him Les, not any variation of grandfather. He was an avid smoker, up to seventy cigarettes a day, and his fingers were stained yellow-brown. He even smoked as he ate.

My paternal grandfather, Henry Tom, started off underground, but when his father died he became a Pearl Insurance agent. He was an Elder in the Presbyterian Church of Wales and the Secretary of Moriah Chapel. He was the only other person in my family who had been active in politics. He was the election agent for Jennie Eirian Davies when she stood for Plaid Cymru in the General Election of 1955 in the Carmarthen con-stituency. That was the first time Plaid Cymru stood in that constituency, which was later to be the seat that gave them their first ever MP, in 1966.

As the 'man from Pearl', my grandfather was respon-sible for going around the houses, collecting money from people. As was the custom in those days, he was referred to as 'Dyn y Pearl' (The Pearl Man). He had to collect from a wide variety of homes and, as you can imagine, that could prove challenging when he had to visit a poor family. My Uncle Howard told me stories of my grandfather going to houses where the baby of the family was in an orange box on the floor, or there were chickens running all over the kitchen table. On one visit to a particular house, he had a rather unexpected welcome. This house had a parrot outside the front door. Every time my grandfather would visit that home, the parrot would say loudly in Welsh, 'Co'r ffycin dyn insiwrans 'na 'to!' ('There's that fucking insurance man again!')

My maternal grandmother died only six years ago, at the good old age of ninety-nine. My children, therefore, knew her well, and they enjoyed a good relationship with their great-grandmother. When she was born, her father wanted to name her after the area of Cardiganshire that he had come from – Aberaeron. There are familiar girls' names linked to that area: Aerona or Aeronwy. The Welsh poet Dylan Thomas's youngest child was christened Aeronwy, following a short period of time Dylan and his wife Caitlin spent in the vicinity during World War II. My great-grandmother decided on Aerona. But she wasn't very good at spelling and so my grandmother was actually christened Eirona. Not only was her name misspelled, but when I came into the world and started to speak, I couldn't pronounce the letter 'r' properly, so I couldn't say her name correctly and any attempt on my behalf to pronounce it sounded like 'Nonna'. So, inevitably, that's what she became known as: Nonna. Which, coincidentally, is the Italian word for grandmother.

Not being able to pronounce the letter 'r' properly didn't only mean that I couldn't pronounce my grandmother's name correctly, but that I couldn't even pronounce my own. If people asked me my name, they would hear me reply 'Cavwyn'. This lasted until I was about seven or eight. It was finally rectified when I was playing with a toy car and my father asked me what it was. My enthusiastic child-like reply was 'carrrrr', making the revving noise of a car at the end of the word. My father responded, 'What did you say? What is it?' I repeated the word with the elongated letter 'r' at the end. 'There we are,' my dad replied, 'you can say it!' From then on, I could say Carwyn.

Moving on to my parents, the pattern continues. One comes from Upper Brynaman, the other from Lower Brynaman. The gene pool is getting smaller! My father was born in 1938, as was my mother. But because they came from different parts of Brynaman, my dad went to Amman Valley Grammar School in Carmarthenshire and my mum went to Ystalyfera Grammar in the Swansea Valley, Glamorganshire. Their school buses would pass each other every day.

My father was born in November 1938 and was the elder of two boys. My uncle, Howard, sadly passed away last year. My dad was given the name Caron Wyn. The name came from one of my grandfather's friends, who had lost a son with the same name. My grandfather also thought that the Reverend Caron Wyn Jones had quite a nice ring to it, but it didn't quite turn out that way!

When my father was at Amman Valley Grammar School, the caretaker there was a former coalminer named David Rees Griffiths. He was more well-known by his bardic name, Amanwy, as he was a prominent Welsh poet and contributed regularly to the local newspapers and to BBC Radio. A film was made about his life for the Festival of Britain. He was also the brother of Jim Griffiths, a Labour MP and the first Secretary of State for Wales. Amanwy's life is a good example of the industrial culture of the area my family came from.

When my dad was seventeen he was given an unconditional offer to go to Loughborough College to study handicrafts and maths. But he wasn't able to take up the offer immediately, as he had to do his National Service first, and he was sent to Germany in 1956 to do his service in the RAF. He was also the first of the family to go into higher education, although his Uncle Edgar had been offered a place to study medicine in Edinburgh, but he was killed in 1942 while serving as an RAF fighter pilot. He was just nineteen.

Near the end of my father's service, when he was home on leave, a telegram arrived saying that he was to be transferred from Mönchengladbach to a records office in England. He had no idea why they were doing this and was mystified by the decision, especially as all his gear was in Germany. His friends had to pack everything for him and send it on to his new base in England. One of his friends made sure that a watch my dad had bought in Germany was also sent ahead. He sliced a bar of soap in half, put the watch inside it and glued it back together again, because they weren't meant to take things home without paying customs duty. Well, this was sixty years ago, so I think we can forget about it now.

The new job was a big change for my dad. The office environment was so completely different to what he'd known, and it took a while for him to settle. It then dawned on him that, as he worked in the records office, he might be able to check on his own records. Maybe then he could see why he had been moved? He didn't expect the explanation he saw when he found his file. In it was a letter from the family GP to the Forces, saying that my dad had to be transferred nearer to his home immediately as his mother did not have very long to live. Nobody had told him that she was so ill. To this day he can remember how his blood chilled when he found out.

In September 1958, my dad finally went to Loughborough and he drove home for Christmas at the end of term. He'd saved some money in the RAF and had bought a thirty-year-old car for £10. He went to speak to his mother, who by that time was nearing the end. When she died the following day, his car horn sounded in the street outside the family home for no apparent reason. He went outside to see what was wrong. But the only way he could silence the horn was by disconnecting the battery. The next time he went to use the car, there was no fault at all with it. When he told his father this, my grandfather's considered reply was, 'Mae clychau'r nefoedd yn galw hi adre!' ('The bells of heaven are calling her home!')

Loughborough didn't offer degrees at that point, so my father left with a diploma rather than a degree. But, over fifty years later, his diploma was upgraded to an honorary degree, together with others who were there at that time. He returned to South Wales to temporary teaching positions in Ystalyfera and Pontardawe before finally obtaining a permanent position in Cathays, Cardiff.

My mother, Katherine Janice, was the elder of two girls. My mum went to Swansea training college and then obtained a teaching position straight after, in Tondu Junior School, in 1958. She stayed at that same school for thirty-three years, even after it moved up the road to Bryncethin.

My parents officially met at the Regal Dance Hall in Ammanford at some time in the 50s, although they were vaguely acquainted before that. They married at Ebenezer Chapel, Brynaman, on 6 April 1963. They were married for forty-six years and they were a good fit for each other. My dad was steady and sensible. He was what I would call a solid character – a definite rock for me as his son. My mum had no time at all for any kind of formality and was one of the world's greatest talkers. My father often threatened to change the name of the house to Nant Siarad (Babbling Brook)! She also knew how to wind people up, with more than a little touch of mischief. One running argument in the family was about the Brynaman Chapels Eisteddfod. My father had always taken great pride in his recitation skills, and still talks of the time when a drama group from Brynaman went to Caernarfon in North Wales and won the National Eisteddfod. My mother would always taunt him by saying that she remembered beating him in a particular recitation competition. To this very day he has always strenuously denied that claim!

Jones. Howells. Lloyd. Hopkin. Walters. Hugh. The only surnames in the family going back for centuries. Every one of these different names in the same family would have been on one colliery list or another in the area. I'm part of the first generation on both sides of my family, going back a long way, not to work in the mines. But even though I didn't work underground, I still feel the need to define myself in terms of my relationship with the coal that was in my ancestors' veins. Maybe, subconsciously, that's what those rattling collecting tins in Bridgend Tesco connected with.

THREE

First Light

I WASN'T BORN where I was supposed to be born. The plan was for me to take my rightful place in the heritage that I've described in the previous chapter, which should have meant that the first light I would see would be that of Carmarthenshire. Such a plan wasn't just a wistful family longing, either. Far from it. By the time my mother was pregnant, my parents had made their home in Bridgend. With my parents teaching in two different places, they had soon come to realize that they needed to set up home in a location that offered a compromise and that lessened the travel for them both. That's why Bridgend was chosen: convenient for my father to go to Cardiff and for my mum to work in Bryncethin, near Bridgend.

But there was no way that I was going to be born there. Plans were made for my mother to go to the Amman Valley Hospital, located near the town of

Ammanford, the nearest town to the three villages so deeply linked to my ancestry. When the time was right, she took her place in that hospital, ready for my birth. My mother, however, soon became unwell. Or rather, I was giving her problems. Days after the due date, and probably later than it should have been, my mother was transferred by ambulance to Morriston Hospital.

The location of that hospital is a moot point. As far as address is concerned, it is in Swansea. But as far as psycho-geography is concerned, it's in Morriston. My father, more than anyone, was acutely aware of such a distinction. For the uninitiated, the Swansea people are called Jacks. Legend has it that this is because of a famous dog, a black retriever called Jack, who rescued twenty-eight people from the sea in the 1930s. His death in 1937 was reported in the press throughout the UK.

The use of the name Swansea Jack has changed over the years since then. For those from outside Swansea, calling someone a Swansea Jack isn't exactly a compliment. That's how my dad saw it as well, and he insisted that I was born in Morriston and that there was no way his son was a Swansea Jack. Morriston. *That* is where his boy was born.

So I was born in Morriston Hospital, wherever that may be! I was a high forceps delivery in the end. I was not well and neither was my mother. My father remembers the doctor coming out into the corridor just before I was born, shaking his head. Things were not good. They couldn't find a heartbeat. My father says that he could feel the blood drain from his body. Once my pulse was found, other complications came to light. I had torticollis, or 'twisted neck', which meant that one side of the neck would grow more slowly than the other. The doctors offered two solutions – either I'd need surgery or my parents would have to manipulate the shorter side of my neck through uncomfortable stretches. My father chose to do the stretches and had to do so for two years.

The pain of these exercises for me was really bad, and I have no doubt that it was an awful thing for him to have to do to his son. An awful thing made worse by the fact that, whenever he came towards me, I would invariably run away from him, in case there was more treatment on the way. It must have been horrible for him to have his child be so scared of him. But if he hadn't done what he did, one side of my neck would be shorter than the other.

When my grandfather came to see us in the special-care unit, his humour bounced well against my mother's jovial attitude towards the tough situation she was in. My mum said, 'You might as well measure me for the slab now.' To which my undertaker grandfather replied,

'My eye is good enough.' My mother was quite ill at the time and was advised not to have another child. That was another issue for my parents to face. They had married four years earlier and had just set up their first home together, only to be told that their firstborn should be their last.

When mother and baby were both strong enough to leave the hospital, I took my place in the family home in Bridgend. It's always been a market town and remained so until the end of the last century, albeit in a weakened condition. No doubt this is largely due to the fact that the town sits just below the confluence of three rivers – the Garw, the Llynfi and the Ogmore. A fourth river, the Ewenny, joins the Ogmore south of the town on its way to the Bristol Channel.

The coming of coal and rail clearly had an impact on Bridgend. But, as already mentioned, the town itself never had a coal mine. So the market trading could continue with little change. The first major change in character for Bridgend was during World War II, when a large munitions factory was built there. At its peak, the factory employed as many as 40,000 people, most of whom were women. These workers were bussed in from many different parts of South Wales, including the villages further west associated with my family. There was also an underground munitions storage depot in the nearby village of Brackla. This was a period of intense activity that brought in many newcomers.

Bridgend also had a prisoner-of-war camp during this time, Island Farm. It was based in buildings originally meant as hostels for workers in the munitions factory. The buildings were used as a base for American soldiers in 1943, and it's said that Eisenhower visited the troops there before they left for France. In 1944, it became a prisoner-of-war camp. One of those imprisoned there was General Gerd von Rundstedt, the Commander in Chief of the German Army in Western Europe. He was taken from Island Farm to the Nuremburg Trials and returned there afterwards. In March 1945, between sixty-seven and seventy prisoners – there is no definitive figure – escaped from Island Farm. This was the largest German escape in the UK, and more German prisoners escaped from Bridgend than the number of British soldiers who fled the Germans at Stalag Luft III, which the film *The Great Escape* was based on. It should be noted, however, that all the Germans who escaped from Island Farm were caught.

With the guns of war silenced and the munitions workers back at their pre-war duties, Bridgend returned to concentrating on market trading once more. The next big change in the town would be the opening of nearby sections of the M4 motorway, from the late 70s onwards.

This led to two big companies settling in the area, Ford and Sony, who have, between them, employed thousands in the area. My most recent political activity as an Assembly member was to be involved in discussions with Ford on their plans to close the Bridgend factory. Unfortunately, they have now taken that decision and up to 1,700 workers will lose their jobs when the factory closes in 2020. Another significant change is on the horizon for Bridgend.

In the late 60s, when I was settling into my new home with my parents, Bridgend market town was my formative environment. The reason that we were there was also indicative of another influence on the town's growth. As well as continuing to be a market town, in recent years Bridgend has developed as a commuter area for people working in Cardiff who want to avoid the hustle and bustle of city living. The rail connection to the capital was well established and the developing M4 would only improve the Bridgend–Cardiff connection. The nearby town of Cowbridge was very similar to Bridgend, and had been for centuries, with both being market towns. But Bridgend owes its growth into a bustling industrial town to those more direct commuter links it has to Cardiff. Cowbridge railway station closed as far back as the pre-Beeching days of 1951.

We lived not far from the town centre. One major

factor in integrating my parents into their new area was the chapel. Coming from a chapel-going tradition back home, they naturally sought to continue to do so when they moved to Bridgend. They had gone to different denominations of chapel in Brynaman, my father being a Presbyterian and my mother a Congregationalist, but both were Welsh-speaking chapels.

On moving to Bridgend, they settled on Tabernacl, the Welsh Congregationalist chapel in town. That proved to be a good move for me as well. When I was all of five years old, the time came for me to recite my first verse of scripture in the Children's Service. I vividly remember being called to stand by the minister, who introduced me by my full name, Carwyn Howell Jones. I stretched to my full height and said, 'Duw Cariad Yw.' ('God is Love'). The minister responded enthusiastically and gave me a verbal pat on the back. My public career standing up to speak in front of people had begun! I have no doubt that being part of the chapel culture gave me the best kind of start in public life.

THE SCHOOL gave me a similar boost. When I was seven, I was narrator in the primary school play. When it came time for me to go to school, there was only one option, really. I went to the school at which my mother taught, not to any of the ones nearest to our home. Such a practice would have been far more acceptable then than it is today. Bryncethin was a working-class village, owing much of its growth to coal and the building of the munitions factory. From its early days, it would have been a predominantly Welsh-speaking village too, closer in culture and ethos to the Brynaman area. This was true of so many of the villages surrounding Bridgend, and those influences were still strong in those villages as the 60s drew to a close.

Many people, particularly Welsh speakers, assume that I was born in my ancestral area because of the way I speak the Welsh language. It has more of the West Walian lilt to it, the rise and fall not heard the further east you travel. My vocabulary also has Brynaman words and sayings. This is because I went to school with my mum. It was an English-medium school, where subjects were not taught in Welsh. But I spoke to my mum in Welsh, and in *her* Welsh. No doubt there would have been a different tone to my mother tongue if I had gone to a school nearer my home.

I loved my school days. I mixed with other children of different backgrounds to myself, which I really enjoyed. Although I didn't mix much with the children closer to home, there were two girls who lived opposite me who both spoke Welsh. That wouldn't make anyone blink in Brynaman, but it was more of a surprise in

Bridgend. One of them, Delyth Morgan, went on to play rugby for Wales in the early days of women's rugby. She was an early pioneer in a game dominated by men and the macho attitude that, in turn, engendered. But most of my friends came from my school.

I then went to the comprehensive school in Bridgend, Brynteg. It was a huge school, with over 1,800 pupils. It's made a particular contribution to the big outside world of rugby: it has produced eight players for the British and Irish Lions, the cream of the cream from Wales, England, Ireland and Scotland. They are Jack Matthews, JPR Williams, Gareth Williams, Mike Hall, Rob Howley, Dafydd James, Gavin Henson and Rhys Webb. Dr Jack Mathews toured with the Lions to New Zealand and Australia in 1950 and was famously described as a cross between a bulldozer and a brick wall. JPR was a member of the magnificent Lions team who secured their first and, to date, only series win against the All Blacks in New Zealand in 1971. Gareth Williams toured South Africa in 1980 and tragically died of multiple system atrophy in 2018. Mike Hall toured Australia with the Lions in 1989, as did Dafydd James in 2001. Rob Howley was on that same tour as well, following a previous tour with the Lions to South Africa in 1997. Rob was also a member of the highly successful Wales coaching team under Warren Gatland.

The colourful, often flamboyant Gavin Henson toured New Zealand in 2005, and Rhys Webb toured the same country in 2017. Forgive the roll call, but I am proud to have been at the same school as such a fine pride of Lions in a rugby-mad country such as Wales.

I must quickly add that I wouldn't have been challenging any of the eight if I had been in school at the same time as them. I was there at the same time as Mike Hall and Rob Howley, and they were in a different league.

I know why the area succeeded in providing such a pedigree of rugby players, though. I have very painful, almost physical, memories of why that is the case. I remember playing as an eight-year-old on a full-size rugby pitch. Standing under the posts at one end of the pitch, looking across towards the other posts. It felt as if I was looking all the way to Cardiff! When I played, of course there weren't any actual posts: they were imaginary, because the facilities weren't there for real ones. So we were toughened up at a young age. Rugby was by far the dominant sport in Brynteg. Cricket was tolerated in the summer months, but football was frowned upon and actively discouraged. 'What do you want to play that game for, boy?' was a very real perceived mantra from every teacher. Football was found, if anywhere, in the boys' clubs outside the school gates.

Moving to the 'big school' when I was eleven had one immediate effect. Most of my primary school friends went to another comprehensive school, in the Ogmore Valley. As I had more friends in my primary school than in the area where I lived, I was now in a situation where those friends from primary days weren't there any more and so I had to make new 'comprehensive' friends in my new school.

When I played the game of rugby at eight years old, I was, surprisingly, chosen to play prop forward. I'm not sure I had the physical attributes to play in such a position then, even though the coach obviously thought so. Certainly, as my first few school years progressed, I grew further and further away from the bulkiness expected of props. I grew lankier, contrary to the family genetic tradition. Rugby still continued, to the level I was able to reach, and I enjoyed it, but it came to a very sudden halt for reasons which had nothing to do with rugby ability.

When I was fourteen, my eyesight, which had deteriorated since I was five years old, got to the stage where I could hardly see anything in front of me at all. Over the years I'd found myself moving closer and closer to the TV to see the programmes properly. It was evidently a gradual deterioration, but by the time I was in form three, it had become serious. It soon got to the point where rugby had to go completely. I just couldn't see enough to play the game. I needed glasses, obviously, and they were really thick glasses, which brought with them so much emotional baggage.

My confidence started to erode, and it wasn't long before it disappeared completely. I felt so self-conscious and I lost any self-respect I might have previously had. Being with other people proved to be very difficult. My academic ability hadn't changed, but it was more and more difficult to express it. Looking back now, I went through what would be described as depression because of my physical condition. I had gone from being a member of the rugby team, who was successful academically and popular with my peers, to being on the outside. Everything I had going for me before was suddenly not there any more. The way I saw myself – the ungainly kid with thick glasses – consumed my thoughts, and I assumed that's how others saw me too, which in turn reinforced all the negative things I thought about myself. It was a vicious emotional circle. No doubt I got to the point where I thought people were thinking things about me that they actually weren't. But you try telling that to a teenager with issues! This situation lasted until I was about sixteen years old, when I got contact lenses. They were a very long two years.

FOUR

A Green Post Box, Militant,
and Some Pubs

BRYNTEG WAS one of the first schools in Wales to offer drama 'O' Level. This, along with some public speaking events at school, gave me something to fill the void that was left by not being able to play rugby any more. I also started listening to music quite a lot. The first music I responded to was punk, when I was moving from primary to secondary school, quickly followed by metal when the punk scene faded after a couple of years. And, of course, there was sport. In those days, Bridgend had a really good rugby team and I would go regularly to the Brewery Field to watch them play. My appreciation of the game wasn't just as an avid spectator, but it was also statistical. I loved the facts and figures that could accumulate with each game, including that old ritual of marking the scores on your match-day programme as the game progressed.

My loss of confidence might well have affected my schoolwork and other aspects of my life, but I did well enough in my exams to think about 'A' Levels. I had studied chemistry, physics and biology for 'O' Level, no doubt because there had been some degree of family influence in wanting me to be a doctor. In the type of community that my parents came from, the doctor was placed high on a pedestal, and I was told repeatedly that I would be a doctor one day. I had good grades in the three sciences at 'O' Level and the original plan was that they would be my 'A' Level subjects as well. But I was unsure as to whether I wanted to take those subjects any further. My heart wasn't really in them. After much discussion with my father, it was decided that I could drop those subjects and take a completely different path for the next stage of my education. Consequently, I did English, economics and history for 'A' level.

I had always loved history. Who knows where these formative interests come from? But I'm sure that there were a few contributing factors that led to my love of history as a child. The area my family came from, as I've described, was steeped in myth and legend, and it was a close community where people would share their own personal histories. I can still recall hearing the stories of one man who had been in the Boer War. Others would tell their stories of the World Wars or of other significant events in their Welsh past. I would hear stories of the soup kitchens of the 20s and speak to men who knew prominent leaders in mining in South Wales, such as Arthur Horner and Arthur Cook. History and politics intertwined in such communities and it was all taken in, almost subconsciously.

In addition, when I was a boy, I was given a book by a primary school head teacher, David Walters, from Llwydcoed. It was H. E. Marshall's *Kings and Things*, which was published way back in 1937. Marshall was famous for publishing the classic, if by now outdated, *Our Island Story: A Child's History of England for Boys and Girls* and *Kings and Things*, both light-hearted introductions to some well-known stories in history, similar up to a point to the *Horrible Histories* series of today. This headmaster's son had read the book and it was then passed on to me. That book lit a spark for me which then led to my doing history 'A' Level.

Both my parents read, and there were always books around at home. Thankfully, reading wasn't a problem for my eyesight, and I continue to be an avid reader. In my school days I loved Alfred Hitchcock books and the *Adventure* series written by Willard Price. They told the adventures of two boys, Hal and Roger. In the first book, *Amazon Adventure*, the boys are eighteen and thirteen and they've taken a year off school to travel the world collecting animals for their father's menagerie back home in Long Island. I enjoyed those stories immensely. I didn't warm to Enid Blyton books at all, I must say.

There was only one type of book that would not be found anywhere at home, or indeed on the shelves of any of my extended family's homes – political books. There was no interest in reading about politics at all. My parents voted at every opportunity, but there was no strong allegiance to one particular party, no campaigning for one cause or another. They came from a certain tradition of Welsh politics, but that wasn't articulated in party terms particularly strongly. Nobody in my family stood to be a councillor or for any other type of election. No one was a paid-up member of a political party. The closest we got to that was my paternal grandfather, who had been an election agent for Plaid Cymru in 1955.

So I started my 'A' Levels. If it was easy to see where the history and the English came from, economics was more of a surprise. It certainly couldn't be traced from any political family influence. But I really enjoyed it. I enjoyed it to the point that, when the time came for me to have that obligatory careers talk in my second year of sixth form, I said I wanted to do an economics degree. When I told the careers teacher of my intention to do economics, his instant reply was: 'Why? All you can do with that is teach.' There was a definite inference that such a path was the academic equivalent of going down the mines, despite the fact that both my parents were teachers.

So the discussion continued and the careers teacher suggested law. I said okay, and that was that. That's how I ended up doing a law degree in Aberystwyth. I fell into it. Leicester, Warwick, UWIST and Keele were my other choices of university, but 'Aber' was very much right at the top. I had been to Aberystwyth so many times with my family as a child, and I had grown to love the place. It was full of good childhood memories and I was keen to spend my student days there.

But before I got there, I basked in the knowledge that I had finally finished school, and the long summer holidays stretched out blissfully in front of me. To make the most of this time off, myself and three friends decided to venture abroad together. Dai Williams, who is a doctor now and would be my best man, Paul Scattergood, who works in Barrow, as an engineer, and Steve Clark, who now lives in Kent. The four of us travelled to Lloret in Spain by bus from Cardiff. This was my own *Adventure* story!

When we got there, we were told that there had been a mix-up with the booking. We had booked two rooms. They asked if the four of us would be willing to share one big room and, for the inconvenience, they would give us some money back. That was a no-brainer and we took the extra cash. I slept on a mattress on the floor for the week, in what was the biggest hotel in Europe at the time. Our mothers had drilled it into us that we weren't supposed to drink the water out there and we dutifully obeyed them. But we didn't have the sense to buy bottled water either. So every morning we were extremely parched. We didn't listen to any instructions, maternal or otherwise, to use suncream. That was only for the 'soft' boys. So it was lying in the sun all day, on the pop and the vodka in the evening, until the local police fired their guns in the air to tell everyone it was time to go to bed. No surprise that I had a touch of sunstroke. I was advised that the liqueur Fernet-Branca would be good for me. Fans of *The Sopranos* might recall Carmela Soprano telling her priest that she was 'having a little Fernet. It settles the system.' Well, it didn't for me! Readers of Jilly Cooper books tell me that some of her characters turn to Fernet as a 'hair of the dog' treatment. Again, not for me! But we had a great time, and it was a great way to end my school days before starting a degree. I might have had to drop out of the rugby scene earlier than I had hoped, but I'd been there long enough to learn the phrase 'what goes on tour, stays on tour'. That applies to holidays too.

*

COME SEPTEMBER 1985, I made my way to Aberystwyth. I was to stay in Pantycelyn halls of residence. That's the traditional accommodation for Welsh-speaking students. It was opened in 1951, and it's where Prince Charles stayed while he learned Welsh before his investiture in 1969, and it has been a centre for much student-based Welsh-language protest, particularly in the 60s and 70s. For me it was, in the first few weeks, a place where I would once again feel a little isolated. I was in a situation where many of the students had come to Aberystwyth from the same comprehensive school, already in tight-knit friendship groups. Just as I started my comprehensive school life as an outsider, the same was happening at the start of my degree days. I was terribly homesick in those early weeks at Aber.

Ironically, the first friend I made there was Dave Taylor, from Coychurch near Bridgend. We had met once before, back home, at a club in the town called Crossways. We were both playing on the fruit machines there, and that is one tradition that continued throughout the Aber days. Dave and I asked the same girl out on the same day and she chose him. I wasn't bitter at all, honest. Soon after meeting Dave, I met Alun Cox, who is now a Plaid Cymru councillor in the Rhondda. We stuck together for all three years.

Pantycelyn was a quaint halls of residence. It was a

definite throwback to years gone by in many ways. A bell would ring at 7.30 every morning to wake us up, and at 8.30 on Sundays. It was a hand bell, with a clanger that would often find itself with a sock tied round it to shut it up. The electrical system was quite possibly prehistoric, with strict instructions given to every student on arrival as to what we were and weren't allowed to plug in. I was there for two years and, despite the early bells and threat of electric shock, it had a certain cosy comfort.

Dave, Alun and I all found it pretty difficult to break into the Pantycelyn scene. Many people already knew each other, and the vast majority were Welsh speakers. This was in stark contrast to my days in the comprehensive. In the sixth form there, only two of us had spoken Welsh. Counter-intuitively, it was a different culture to the one I was used to, even though the language was the same.

Everyone was friendly enough; there was absolutely no animosity. But we were never accepted as part of the crowd. Perhaps we didn't make enough of an effort? Dave doesn't speak Welsh at all, so it was even more difficult for him to break through. Consequently, we socialized primarily outside of our halls of residence. This also meant that we got to know other halls of residence fairly well as our social network grew.

Not only was I in Aberystwyth – which has always

been, and continues to be, a very Welsh town in terms of language and culture – but I was staying in the Welsh-language halls of residence, regarded as a hotbed of Cymdeithas yr Iaith Gymraeg (Welsh Language Society) activity. Some of their members tended to regard members of Plaid Cymru as too soft in their approach to nationalistic issues. The post box outside Pantycelyn was forever being painted green and then being painted back red again. I'm sure the paint was thicker than the post box itself!

Alongside this, there was a totally separate Students' Union for Welsh speakers, UMCA. No official from the main Students' Union could be considered for any role in UMCA, even if they spoke Welsh. During my time there, a student called Alun Davies was expelled from UMCA when they discovered that he had been an official in the Students' Union. He was very active with Plaid Cymru then, but even that couldn't stop him getting thrown out of UMCA. Today, he is the Labour Assembly Member for Blaenau Gwent.

It's in these circumstances that I joined the Labour Party. There's no escaping that the party I was joining had a bad reputation in terms of its attitude to the Welsh language and culture. For many in the Labour Party, there was a clear split between nationalism and socialism. The fight for better living conditions for working people in Cardiff, Glasgow and Stoke united people more than any accident of geography did. MPs such as Leo Abse, Ioan Evans, George Thomas and, later, Neil Kinnock would see things that way. But there were other leading Labour MPs in Wales who saw no tension at all in arguing for greater devolution for Wales within the party ranks. It was the Labour Party who campaigned for years to establish a Secretary of State for Wales, and it was a Labour Government that eventually created such a Cabinet post in 1964.

I saw no problem at all in supporting Labour as a passionate Welshman, even in the middle of the sea of nationalistic Welshness I was immersed in. Every generation of my family has spoken the language going back a long, long time. My children speak Welsh, and my wife has learned the language too. I enjoy all aspects of Welsh culture and I champion my Welsh identity continually. I always have. Arriving at Aber with a DNA such as mine was important to me, and it gave me a sense of pride. I was aware of the anti-Welsh label that had been stuck on Labour for decades before that. But, as far as I was concerned, I was not signing up to a religion where I would have to accept all its tenets. I signed up to the basic Labour principles, knowing that there were some things I didn't agree with. The party most able to deal with the issues that had awakened me politically was the

Labour Party. That was it for me. That's where the political battles could be fought, both for living conditions and devolution alike.

I turned up for my first meeting of the Aberystwyth Labour Party at the university and discovered that it was controlled by Militant. The Militant Tendency was a Trotskyist group within the Labour Party, formed in 1965. They had disappeared completely by 1992, so my years in Aber were pretty much their end years.

From 1975 until the mid-80s, Militant and Labour were in a constant battle against each other, amid accusations from the party that Militant members were trying to infiltrate the parliamentary party in order to enforce its more radical left-wing agenda. Eventually, after a long and bitter struggle, the Labour National Executive banned Militant from Labour and some of its members were expelled from the main party. During the Labour Conference of 1985 – my first year as a student, and the first conference after I joined the party – Labour leader Neil Kinnock denounced Militant publicly from the platform.

Rumours of their decline were certainly exaggerated in Aberystwyth, but there were students in that branch who did not endorse the Militant standpoint. I was one of them. By the end of that year, at the AGM, a few of us put ourselves up for election against some of the Militant officials. That was my first taste of standing for election. I lost, but the process had started! Other than that, there wasn't a great deal of political activity on my part during my first year. I went to meetings regularly enough, but there were no campaigns or protests as such to throw myself into, and there wasn't a General Election that year to allow me to get involved in any campaigning.

Over the years, lots of people have asked me why, as a passionate Welshman and Welsh speaker, I didn't join Plaid Cymru. It's true that I read a lot of literature by those connected with the party, but it put me off. My grandfather worshipped Gwynfor Evans, the first Plaid MP, but his views of a pacifist, temperant Wales fighting against oppression just didn't chime with reality for me.

There *was* a General Election in June 1987, however, and that meant that I could actively canvas for the party in Aberystwyth. In that 1987 election, there was a change of MP in the Cardiff West Constituency that would have a bearing on my future political role. The incumbent Conservative MP, Stefan Terlezki, lost his seat to a certain Rhodri Morgan. Rhodri served his constituency for many years before becoming an Assembly Member and then First Minister. But as a second-year law student in Aber that year, I can safely say that there was not a single thought in my mind that I would be in politics, let alone working with Rhodri.

There were very few restaurants in the town then, so student life pretty much revolved around the pubs of Aberystwyth. This might have been the mid-to-late-80s, but all the pubs in the county of Ceredigion still closed on a Sunday. Sunday closing was introduced in Wales back in the 1880s. It came from within the Liberal Party and was driven by the prominent Welsh Nonconformists in its ranks, among them future Prime Minister David Lloyd George. Gladstone's Liberal Government passed the Sunday Closing (Wales) Act in 1881. That 'Wales' in parenthesis is significant. This Act was the first Wales-only Westminster legislation passed since the Acts of Union in 1536 and 1543. At the time, the majority of people in Wales were chapel-going Nonconformists, but the Welsh minority who considered themselves Church of England, as it was then called in Wales, enjoyed privilege and status denied to chapel people. Many people were taken to court for refusing to pay the tithe, the tax due to the Church, including my own great-grandfather. The Welsh wanted a fairer system, so the passing of the Sunday Closing Act gave Wales a distinct identity, which historians have argued established principles that eventually led to devolution.

For us as students in 'dry' Ceredigion, it just meant that we couldn't have a pint in a pub on a Sunday. But the Students' Union was open, and many of the town's clubs offered Sunday membership. One of these was the Squash Club in North Parade. There were courts there, but I never saw anyone playing on Sunday. The bar was a better attraction, and, unsurprisingly, the club closed not long after the pubs were allowed to open on a Sunday. Sunday closing also encouraged journeys out of county to neighbouring 'wet' counties and, as such, we were able to broaden our education, you could say. This led to a rather bizarre situation in one village not far from my family roots. One pub in Cwmtwrch, The George, crossed the boundary between three counties; one county with Sunday closing, the others without. This meant that part of the pub could open on a Sunday but part of it was closed! The Act was repealed in 1961, with each county given the right to hold a referendum on whether it wanted its pubs to open on Sunday or not. Ceredigion didn't vote in favour until as late as 1989, the last but one county in the UK allow Sunday opening. The last was Dwyfor, which stayed dry until 1996.

Not to give the impression that it was all drink, we did have Theatr y Werin in Aberystwyth, which was a popular attraction. The big amusement arcade on the seafront, The King's Hall, had closed down by the time I was a student, and I had to be satisfied with my fond memories of spending hours there when I was a child on holiday. By my third year, I had started to play rugby again. Not for the university, but in the Digs League, and I played for Cwrt Mawr halls of residence. I wasn't in residence there, but that's who I played for, because that's where a lot of my mates were. We called ourselves the Cwrt Mawr 1st XV. There wasn't a 2nd XV.

While I was here, the Cwrt Mawr rugby team arranged a trip to Ireland to see the Wales *v.* Ireland Five Nations game in March 1988. It was organized by Steve Williams from Pontarddulais, the team captain. It was advertised in official university circles as a shopping trip, which meant that it could be subsidized. Good start! There were two people on the bus who were actually going shopping, all the others weren't. We left Aber on a Friday after stop-tap. Steve had decided that he didn't fancy stopping here, there and everywhere for the boys to go to the toilet, so he brought two big containers with him, the kind used by caravanners to hold water. By Machynlleth, barely thirty miles on, they were both full. That's what comes from leaving after stop-tap. For those in the younger generation, stop-tap was the time at which pubs had to close by law, usually 11 p.m.

We got to Holyhead for the ferry and, by then, a lot of us were feeling tired and starting to nod off. But once on the ferry, if you were caught napping, Ollie Bromham from Bryncoch would shout 'No sleeping on tour!' at you. When we got to Dublin, at about six in the morning, we were all ready to leave the ferry – all but one. Ollie had fallen asleep and we had to find him and then wake him up. What a pleasure that was!

After breakfast in McDonald's on a lovely sunny day in Dublin, we walked the streets looking for a pub that was open. There weren't any, of course. So we went round the back of one we found, knocked on the door and asked them if we could come in. Luckily, they were happy to oblige with good old Irish hospitality. It's a pub I know very well by now, called O'Donoghue's. We stayed there until match time. That was good too, because Wales beat Ireland to claim the Triple Crown, their first in eight years. Paul Moriarty, Paul Thorburn and a 'Jiffy' drop goal secured a 12–9 victory for us. Wales shared the Five Nations Championship with France that year, the last time the championship was shared. Since then, if two teams are equal on points at the top of the table, other factors come into the equation in order to decide on one outright winner. The first try scorer was Terry Kingston, the Ireland hooker, and he was my sweepstake number. He won me £50, a goodly sum in those days.

The boys went back to O'Donoghue's after the match and from there to the ferry, and then on to the bus back to Aber, where we arrived Sunday morning. We had a great couple of days away – totally draining and exhausting, but good fun. But if you suggested such a schedule to me today, I might as well order my coffin straight away. We still talk of having a reunion game involving the boys on that tour. But with all of us hovering either side of fifty, that reunion game is increasingly likely to be a game of bowls.

After two years in Pantycelyn, six of us moved into a house together on North Parade. Dave, Alun and myself, plus Lewis, a geology student from Huntingdon, Fiona, a drama student from the North-East of England, and Liz, a zoology student from Chesterfield. We lived in a flat above a dentist. There was no heating there but the electricity was included in the price, so we all had convector heaters. That was a great year and we all got on well.

People ask me what makes Aber special and I can only respond that it's the friends you make for life. When we all turned fifty, there were a number of parties and many of the boys hadn't been together for many years. But it was as if we'd only met up last week. Early in 2019, we had a small dinner for a few of us in Bridgend. We were joined via FaceTime by Tim Stokes, who lives in Ireland, and Alan Troy, now a judge in Australia, who was slightly bewildered by being contacted at breakfast time by a bunch of not wholly sober middle-aged men. We wanted them with us even though they were miles away.

Friends for life, that's what it gave me. All of our closest friends are still those who we knew then. One of them, Ian Herbert, had left by the time I arrived at Aber, but people spoke of his escapades with awe. Eventually I got to meet this legend!

And I had a few girlfriends while I was there, but I should also mention that on my course there was a dark-haired Belfast girl. We didn't speak during all the time we were there, but she was to come back into my life in a few years.

FIVE

Broadcasting, the Bar and
the Dog and Duck

BY THE TIME I left Aber, I had become the Chair of the Labour Party group in the university. I had settled comfortably on the centre left of the party, supporting Neil Kinnock's way of looking at politics. I also became Vice-President of External Affairs at the Students' Union.

During this time, I had my first opportunity to contribute to a TV programme. One of the dominant issues of the day was AIDS (Acquired Immune Deficiency Syndrome). It hadn't been long since it had become a phenomenon that had gripped everyone, with a real fear among those who didn't have it and a stigma attached to those who did. The condition was first identified in 1981, but it really hit public awareness in the mid-80s. There was genuine panic about it, because little was known about how it spread and there was no hope of a cure at all in those days. Although both men and women, gay or straight, could be affected by the virus, it quickly became associated with the gay community in particular. One of the first high-profile deaths through AIDS happened not long after I started at Aber: the screen idol Rock Hudson died of the disease in October 1985.

S4C, the Welsh-language Channel 4, wanted to make a programme about how the spread of AIDS had affected young people's attitude towards sex. Their current affairs series, *Y Byd ar Bedwar* (The World on Four), approached the college to ask for students who were willing to contribute. I was more than happy to do so. A great deal of my work as Vice-President of External Affairs involved dealing with AIDS-related issues. It was therefore a natural step for me to take part in the programme. Myself, and the others taking part in the discussion, were prepared for it in the afternoon before the evening recording (mainly through HTV – Harlech Television, the ITV franchise for Wales – taking us to the Cŵps pub for a few hours!)

I told my family that I was going to be on TV and my grandmother duly informed everyone in her chapel on the first Sunday after I'd let her know. She proudly told everyone: 'Carwyn's on *Byd ar Bedwar* next week!' At the end of the *Byd ar Bedwar* programme the week before the one I was on, they announced what was on the week after. They simply said: 'Next week we shall be talking to young people about their attitude towards sex.' That was it! The phone rang and a distraught grandmother was on the other end, beside herself and berating the fact that she had already told everyone that I was to be on TV, only to then find out that we would be talking about such a thing as *sex*. Puritanical sensibilities were duly riled and my grandmother was mortified beyond belief!

One of the questions we were asked during the programme was related to how our families had reacted to the fact that we were contributing to the topic under discussion. I said that I had talked it through with my parents and they were fine about it. But, I said, I wasn't sure how my grandmother would react. Another phone conversation ensued. She was delighted that I had mentioned her publicly on air! So much so, in fact, that I was evidently forgiven, as far as any perceived shame in the eyes of her fellow chapel-goers was concerned. Indeed, she elaborated: 'Things have changed now, of course, haven't they? It's not like it was in my day.' The power of television!

For me, my first TV appearance was over. That added to the early Sunday School appearances and the school drama and public-speaking opportunities in honing my presentation and public appearance skills.

*

I LEFT ABER in 1988, with a 2:2 in Law. I was more than happy with that, because I didn't particularly want to throw myself into the subject or follow where it could lead. I was happy to do just enough to get me to the next stage, whatever that might be, and I had not used my long summer holidays to find any law-related summer job. During those holidays, '86 and '87, I instead worked for the Welsh Joint Education Committee, the WJEC. My job was to check the envelopes containing marked scripts that came back from examiners. We checked that all the scripts were in the envelope and then filed them.

After I finished uni in 1988, the original intention was to become a solicitor. But I decided to study for the Bar instead. I think I decided to go in that direction because I was pretty good at thinking on my feet and comfortable speaking in front of people in a formal situation. It appealed to me more than the day-to-day aspects involved in a solicitor's work. I also knew that I didn't want to go into politics immediately, as I thought it was important to have experience in the broader world of employment. In fact, from 1988 to about 1993, I was not politically active at all.

I went to Gray's Inn, London, to train for the Bar. In those days it was free for those of us who came from mid-Glamorgan. So there were no major financial considerations to think about at all in making the decision. Living costs were required, of course, but I was fortunate enough to stay in a building erected by the Corporation of London to thank people from the Colonies for their contribution to the World Wars. It was open to postgraduate students not born in England. So I was there as a representative of the Welsh 'colony'!

In those days, in addition to the lectures and the necessary exams, one essential formal requirement was to attend twenty-four dinners at Gray's Inn. For a dinner to count as officially one of the twenty-four, you had to put your gown on and be in the hall by 7 o'clock, when the door would shut. No one was allowed in after that. Arrive late and the dinner didn't count. The Benchers would take their place on the top table and, after grace was said, the three-course meal was served. We always thought of the Benchers as old but distinguished barristers. I'm one myself now, which is a great honour, and I no longer think of them as old. There was also a lot of wine involved. At 8 o'clock, things would come to a halt and the door would open, but many of us then stayed on for debates or a simple sing-song, led, of course, by the sizeable group of Welsh students there.

Quite often, later on during those evenings, there would be a debating event. I soon got involved in these, to the point of teaming up with a colleague of mine, Richard Hitchcock, to compete as a duo in the debating competitions. We competed in London and also in other universities around England. The opportunity then came for us to travel to a competition at Princeton University, New Jersey. Our first competition was against Yale. They evidently took the whole thing very seriously, as they had a coach for their team, who was instructing them as if his team were about to take part in an international rugby match. Our preparation was more along the lines of how fans approach an international – we turned up after a few beers! The style of debating was different to what we were accustomed to, and it took a bit of getting used to as well. We were given topics which were pretty obscure, to be honest, and it wasn't the Oxford Union motion format. But it was an invaluable experience, as well as a really good time.

At the end of the competition, there was a social event. At some point in the evening, a lad started to sing 'Sosban Fach', a rugby song known throughout the rugby-playing world. It was quite bizarre to hear it in Princeton during a debating competition event. I introduced myself to the singer, and I gathered that he was there as part of the Durham University debating team. His name was Robert Buckland, he is now the Conservative MP for South Swindon, and, until 2019, he was the Solicitor General in the Conservative Government. Robert was born and bred in Llanelli, hence his rendition of 'Sosban Fach', the unofficial anthem of the Llanelli Scarlets rugby team. He showed early political promise in his hometown when he won a seat on Dyfed County Council for one of the Llanelli wards, and in doing so became the first Conservative to win any kind of seat for many a year in staunchly Labour Llanelli. Rob and I practised together at the Swansea Bar for a few years and he had a good reputation as a barrister and also as a mimic. He's Lord Chancellor now and has done well.

I WAS IN LONDON for a year. One thing I was happy I was able to do while I was there was to continue playing rugby. I played college rugby and I went to a training session for London Welsh, but on arrival I soon realized that their approach to the game was for those who took it seriously, not someone like me, who wanted a spare-time activity. So that didn't last long!

I attained the necessary qualifications in Gray's, including attending all twenty-four formal dinners. I then headed to Cardiff to begin my pupillage, the final stage of barrister training, which is vocational. I shared a house in Tydfil Place, which is in the Roath area of Cardiff. That unusual Roath name probably goes as far back as the Brythonic language and refers to ramparts. There are similar place names in Ireland. Tydfil was a

Welsh martyr, who gave her name to the former industrial capital of Wales – Merthyr Tydfil. These days, as it
was when I was there, the area is a mix of large affluent
Victorian houses, student accommodation and ethnic
minority communities. I shared a house with predominantly medical students. We didn't trash the place, to be
fair to us, but equally we didn't know the meaning of the
word 'cleaning'. We had plenty of parties and there were
always random people staying there for a few nights at
a time. Needless to say, many of those who were more
on the wild side in those student days are top consult-
ants and surgeons today. There was a Med Club in the
grounds of the Heath Hospital, which we went to on a
Friday. I won't mention some of the things I saw there,
but 'work hard, play hard' was definitely the medics'
motto.

As far as my own career was concerned, I hadn't
settled on any one particular area of law as my spe-
cialty at this point. Pupillage lasts twelve months, at the
end of which you are eligible to apply for a full-time
position, known as a tenancy. After six months in Newport, I secured that tenancy at the Gower Chambers in
Swansea. So that meant I was to move to yet another
city, this time the one where I was born – if, unlike my
father, you accept that Morriston Hospital is in Swansea.
There was no point in me staying in Cardiff and com-

muting, because, even as recently as that, there was no M4 motorway all the way between Cardiff and Swansea.

In those very early days as a barrister, I knew deep down that my working life wasn't going to be entirely spent practising law. I just wasn't committed enough. I had achieved the necessary qualifications at every stage, so it wasn't a question of ability. I also did enjoy my days as a barrister. It wasn't as if they were endless days of drudgery. But I knew that there was something else out there for me. Still, I made some good friends in practice. For years I shared a room with two of them, Dean Pulling and Peter Maddox. It's a wonder we did any work because the banter was top class.

Politics was one obvious possibility. Apart from any student political activity, I had been canvassing in the Bridgend area during the 1987 General Election. I joined the Labour candidate Win Griffiths' team, distributing leaflets on the streets of the town. He won that year, beating the incumbent Conservative, Peter Hubbard-Miles.

In 1991, though, there was an incident that was to change my life. I'd arranged to meet a group of friends in the Dog and Duck pub in Cardiff, not far from where the Principality Stadium is now. The Dog and Duck isn't there any more, and is often cited as one of the many sorely missed pubs in Cardiff. One or two of the group

I went to meet were not so much friends, more acquaintances. One member of the group looked familiar. I had spotted her during my very early days in Aberystwyth. She was studying law, just as I was. But despite that link, we weren't in the same group of friends. Now, a mutual acquaintance had led the two of us to the Dog and Duck so many years later. We spoke that evening for the first time. She turned to me and said, 'Is being Welsh important to you, Carwyn?' Not the most obvious icebreaker, perhaps, and, to be honest, I was surprised that she knew my name, but we kept in touch after that. Her name was Lisa Murray.

Lisa is from Northern Ireland and from a large family. Her mother, Stella, is one of seven and her father, Eddie, one of ten (three of whom died in infancy). She is one of four, with an older brother, Paul, sister, Berna, and a younger sister, Rebecca. They were brought up in North Belfast as Catholics. Her father was from the Falls Road and, after a life spent in the furniture business, was at that time measuring and fitting carpets and curtains for schools. In one way you could say he ended up being a casualty of the peace process that ended the Troubles in Northern Ireland. When peace was established, many big companies from outside Northern Ireland moved in and took over businesses that were up until then in more local hands. When this happened to his particular business, Lisa's dad decided to retire. Lisa's mother was a teacher at Star of the Sea boys' primary school, while Lisa went to the girls' school. Although the same school, in theory, the boys and girls were taught in separate buildings, several streets apart, in the New Lodge area of Belfast, a well-known Republican district.

Despite us both attending schools where our mothers taught, Lisa's account of her school days is completely different to my experience in Bryncethin. While my mother received gifts of chocolates and toiletries, Lisa's mother, in addition to such welcome presents, received stray rubber bullets picked up from the street and white cotton hankies embellished by pupils whose fathers were being held in the 'Kesh'. It was not unusual for Lisa and her classmates to hear gunfire on the streets around the school on occasions, or to be evacuated because a nearby pub had been blown up, the flames licking at the school windows. Also, at the beginning of any school day, when calling the register, the teacher would be told a particular pupil was absent that morning because the house had been 'raided and then lifted by the Brits' the night before. In one bizarre incident outside the boys' school, during a gun battle, the IRA hijacked the school dinner van. Lisa's mother and her colleague, Miss Regan, spread the word that the teachers were not amused. Later that day, two men in balaclavas visited the school, heads hung in shame, to apologize and return the van. They had probably been pupils there.

Lisa came from Belfast to study in Aberystwyth because she had some friends who were already there. After finishing her degree, a year teaching in Spain, and doing a postgrad diploma, she settled in Cardiff, and I'm really glad she did. Otherwise, we would never have met again.

After the Dog and Duck reintroduction, the relationship grew. Lisa was living in Cardiff, working for an international exams board, and I was practising in Swansea.

We both knew early on that we would stay together, although we didn't admit as much until later. Our early courtship was mostly me travelling down to Cardiff at weekends, nights out with our mutual friends, ending up in Clwb Ifor, Kiwis or the Taurus, and Sunday afternoon runs into the countryside. The more time we spent together, swapping family stories, talking about our favourite books, films, plays, places we'd love to visit, the best things to eat, the more we knew it was inevitable that we would become committed to each other.

We decided to move in together and buy a house. The most convenient place for both of us was in the Bridgend area, which was equidistant to both work places. We bought a house in the village of Coity on the outskirts of the town. The village has a rather splendid castle, built by one of the famous Twelve Knights of Glamorgan. Our home in the village was a small but lovely stone cottage, with a large garden, a goldfish pond, rose bushes and quite a few trees.

We got to know each other's families. Me, the only child with two first cousins, and her with three siblings and thirty-odd cousins. I finally met the last of them in 2018, twenty-four years after we were married. The first time I went to Belfast was an eye-opener for me. We crossed the border at Newry and drove through a concrete bunker where a soldier noted our number plate. There were police and army roadblocks outside Belfast and a helicopter hovered in the air all day. It looked like an armed camp. Lisa grew up in the city throughout the Troubles and, for her, it was normal. Those days are mainly gone now, hopefully for ever. I had a wonderful welcome from Lisa's parents and have always felt part of the family

We moved in together before we were married. Such a statement these days hardly seems worth noting. But even in the early 90s, that was a big step and one that was not without controversy. We were the first generation in either family to do so. It could have caused a lot of consternation for both families, with the weight of religious and cultural mores bearing heavily on the reaction. In a way, it was more palatable for Lisa's family, as they were in Northern Ireland and far enough away for it not to be on their doorstep. When one of Lisa's uncles, who was a priest, came to stay, lots of suitable and vaguely believable rearrangements had to be made. My grandmother told everyone that we were 'lodging together' in order to save money. The biggest surprise for me was the response from my parents. They lived close by and knew exactly what the situation was. They didn't object at all. But one day, when my father was away with his work as an exams officer in the WJEC, I asked my mum to come for dinner with us and then stay over, because I knew that she didn't like being alone. 'No, it's okay,' she said, 'I'd better not. People might think I approve.'

It was the most natural thing in the world for us to get married, but I wanted to propose in style. I arranged a day trip to Iceland and I proposed to her in Reykjavik. I'm so glad she said yes, as the flight back would have been very difficult otherwise. We went back twenty-five years later, to the Café Paris where I proposed, and we were seated at the same table. I have to say that I was wearing the same sweater that I'd worn that day, even though it had frayed a little. It still fits though!

We had planned to get married the following year. But before that could happen, I knew that I should ask

Lisa's father for his permission to marry his daughter. That meant a visit to Belfast. When we arrived I played a little trick on him. We'd flown to Belfast without telling anyone. I had a very basic mobile phone at the time, a huge house-brick of a thing. Lisa and I stood outside her parents' house and she phoned her mother from there. We rang the doorbell and her father answered. It took him a while to work out what was happening. Lisa then walked upstairs, still talking to her mother, who asked if she was 'on that mobile, there's an echo on the line', not realizing that Lisa was standing right outside the bedroom.

When the shock of the surprise had died down, I explained the reason for our visit and asked her father for Lisa's hand in marriage. He stood bolt upright and reached out his hand to me, saying excitedly, 'Thank you! Thank you!' I was really puzzled by his response. What was he actually thanking me for? Was there something I didn't know? Was he *that* glad to get rid of his daughter? None of that, thank goodness! He was just really grateful for the gesture. When Lisa's younger sister's husband-to-be, Paul, did the same thing, legend has it that my father-in-law responded, 'Thank God!' So it could have been worse.

Later that day, the two mothers spoke to each other, and my mother, not one for diplomacy, told Stella that she had been delighted when we announced that we were getting engaged because she had been afraid we were going to tell them that Lisa was pregnant. This did not go down well with my devout future mother-in-law. Thankfully, they became the best of friends and over the years thoroughly enjoyed each other's company.

Lisa's parents thought that it would be unwise for us to get married in Belfast. The Troubles were still raging, after all, although the first ceasefire was only months away. However, her parents thought that it wasn't safe for a large group of people from Wales and England to gather in Belfast, particularly those of my friends who measured well over six feet in height. They were afraid of them going into the city centre and maybe entering the wrong pub at the wrong time. There were still very visible signs of the conflict in some areas, in terms of concrete barricades, military police, British soldiers, helicopters and city-centre checkpoints. This, of course, was normal day-to-day life for everyone who lived in Belfast. When Lisa first arrived in Aberystwyth, and went into a shop for the first time, she automatically opened her bag and waited to be searched. As it turned out, the official ceasefire in Northern Ireland was signed in August 1994, but by then our plans for getting married in December of that year were well under way. We got married in December 1994 in St Mary's Church,

Bridgend the last couple to be married in the old church building, not the new one that's there now.

Lisa was the first of her siblings to be married, so it was her mother's first time being mother-of-the-bride. Stella has never been a lover of hats or one to overdress for any occasion. She was finally cajoled into compromising with suitably chosen winter wedding attire – a green woollen blazer with a tartan skirt and a baker boy's hat perched at a jaunty angle on her blonde bob. As a line-up formed outside the church, post ceremony, one of the guests, a friend of my mother, approached my mother-in-law to shake her hand and politely asked, 'And is this your national costume?' Suffice it to say, the outfit in its entirety swiftly found itself adorning a shop-window dummy in the local St Vincent de Paul's on my mother-in-law's return home.

At the reception in Coed Y Mwstwr, more of the guests managed to offend her again, but thankfully only slightly. They decided to run a sweepstake on the length of the speeches. Mine was nineteen minutes and one second. The best man's speech was twenty-three minutes and twenty-five seconds. When she found out they'd opened a book, she was horrified there'd been gambling.

Before the wedding, I rang up the Welsh Rugby Union to check that the date, the 3rd of December, didn't clash with the forthcoming Wales *v.* South Africa game. Fortunately, it was the week after. Lisa was appalled that I'd even checked. It did, however, clash with the Barbarians *v.* South Africa game and, sure enough, many of the wedding guests gathered around a black-and-white portable to watch it, much to Lisa's annoyance.

As for a stag night? Well, I did have one in Aberystwyth. Let's just gloss over that. Ritual humiliation, best forgotten. Lisa's hen night was in Cardiff, and her friend Sara took a video camera, so it's captured for ever. It was more civilized (just) than my experience in Aber.

We went to Mexico for our honeymoon, spending ten days just outside Cancún and four days in Mexico City. We arrived back home on the 19th of December and were straight into our first Christmas as a married couple. That was a wonderful period for the two of us.

SIX

Some Politics and Bad Blood

LIFE FOR ME THEN was all about settling down. The pieces were falling into place. I had a job, I was married and we had a home together. Naturally, we started talking about having children. Lisa was one of four and I was an only child. We wanted children of our own for different reasons, maybe, but we were united in the desire to start a family and that was very much a focus for those early days of marriage. We were both twenty-seven when we got married, so maybe age concentrated the mind a little as well.

Against this domestic backdrop, and my lack of conviction that law was actually a long-term career for me, my interest in politics was reignited. That turned out to be on a local level, close to home. I stood as a councillor in the village where we had set up our marital home. There were local elections in 1995 and the local Labour Party asked me to stand in the two-member ward of

Coity Higher. The ward included the village of Coity together with the 1970s community of Litchard and the 1920s community of Pendre, as well as the Princess of Wales Hospital. Prior to that, they had actually asked me if I wanted to stand in a by-election, but that was way too soon for me. I was, however, more than happy to stand in the local authority contest. I won, and my political activity began in earnest. I was the youngest councillor by far on the local authority, the next youngest was a good ten years older than me. Much of politics is about being in the right place at the right time, and that was certainly true for me in 1995. Being a councillor taught me a great deal about the machinery of politics. It taught me about the structures, the networks and the procedures that make local government work. It was a really good grounding.

Our first wedding anniversary was approaching, and Lisa and I knew that we wanted to celebrate it properly. We had a little help. The hotel where our wedding had been held was owned by Virgin at the time, so when it was all paid for, we had quite a lot of bonus air miles as a result. We worked out that we had enough to take one of us for free to New York. So that's where we went. We booked into a hotel that I wouldn't recommend to anyone. The bar downstairs was full of older men with much younger women, shall we say. I walked down the corridor one day and the door to one of the rooms was open. I looked in and there was a man in there, snorting a line of cocaine. Unsurprisingly, Lisa hasn't allowed me to forget where I took her for our first anniversary. All I can say is that this was in the days before Expedia and Tripadvisor.

At that time, Lisa had started a new job at Cardiff University, which required travel. She had been to Madrid with work the week before we went away to New York, and after spending Christmas and New Year in Belfast and Donegal, Lisa became increasingly tired. We put that down to a new job and all the travelling in such a short space of time. Then, at the beginning of the new year, her gums began to bleed quite heavily. She was due to go back to Spain again quite soon, so she needed to get it looked at. As she was still registered with a dentist in Belfast at that point, I suggested that she went along to the Dental School at the university in Cardiff for a check-up. She did so and they suggested a blood test. They also noticed the small purple dots on her chest. She rang my mother while I was at work in Swansea and told her that she was in hospital. She had an abnormal blood count and they wanted to know why. My mother's immediate thought was that 'abnormal blood count' could only mean one thing: cancer. Lisa hadn't considered it and I didn't mention it. When my mother finally got hold of me, I just jumped in the car and bombed along the M4 to the University Hospital of Wales in the Heath, Cardiff.

I was met by an Iranian consultant, who talked me through what he thought Lisa had. When I arrived, he asked me to sit down. I told him I'd rather stand and then he said, 'You'd better sit down.' He told me Lisa had a cancer of the blood. I asked if it was leukaemia and he confirmed it. Even though I had guessed as much and thought about it all the way along the M4, hearing it out loud meant actually acknowledging it for the first time ever. I was stunned and couldn't speak. My parents had arrived by now and my father asked if it was treatable. The consultant said that it was. The fact she was young, he said, and the type of leukaemia she had, made it far more likely that it could be treated. She had an even chance of surviving. At this point Lisa herself still didn't know. When she was told, she was dumbfounded, but it was of some comfort that the doctors suggested that treatment and remission were possible. In the middle of the darkness, those words were clung to out of all proportion to how realistic they actually were.

Back home that night, I walked in through the door and it was as if everything in my own house was in black and white. Everywhere I looked the colour had been drained out of everything. I was alone in our home. Lisa was alone in a hospital bed. But we were both sharing the same worry and concern. Both of us were trying to come to terms in our own way with the 'C word' forcing its way into our lives. It might well be a word we hear, day in, day out, but it doesn't mean anything until it comes to live with you. Lisa, of course, was facing it in a way that I wasn't. She was the one who would undergo the treatment, suffer its awful side effects, and stare down her own mortality. She had only just turned twenty-nine.

The following morning was the beginning of a new sort of life. It was going to be a long haul. Lisa was in and out of hospital for eight months and I visited her every day bar one. There was a regular pattern of travel between Swansea, Bridgend and Cardiff during those months. I carried on with work as best I could. But with such a schedule, I soon began to lose some work in chambers, as I couldn't devote enough time to some of my clients. For me, personally, there was no alternative. I had great support from Lisa's family and from my own. Lisa's two sisters had trained as nurses and, despite neither of them being very tall or physically imposing, they are not to be messed with. They came to stay, as did my parents-in-law, and were a great help and comfort to me as well, as they were able to explain what was happening on the medical side.

The daily reality such a situation creates is actually quite unreal. It's all about living on autopilot through days that give you fog one moment and haze the next. Every silver lining has a cloud. Priorities change. Lisa was going through extensive treatment and all that brought with it. I would regularly speak to patients on the ward one day and come in the following day to find they had died during the night. Thankfully, things have improved hugely since then. After her first chemotherapy, she developed a nasty infection. For some days it was touch and go if she would make it or not. But then she rallied and was ready for more chemotherapy. After the second lot, she became very ill. She also became very uncommunicative. She looked okay, but she wouldn't speak or respond to anyone talking to her. She was like that for a few days. When she came out of it, she didn't remember anything about it.

Lisa had actually gone into remission after the first session of chemotherapy, but that had to be backed up by following the treatment regime. In between treatments she was allowed to go home on condition that, if her temperature spiked above 38.5°, she had to be taken back into hospital, whatever time of day or night.

But the good days weren't signs of full recovery. It got to the point where we were told that the best hope for it to be completely cured was to have a bone marrow transplant. Her two sisters were in Wales at the same time, visiting, so decided to be tested. Multiple test tubes of blood were taken from each and sent away to be analysed, but sadly neither suited. Rebecca then returned to Belfast, took a blood sample from Paul, their older brother, and brought it back on the plane to Wales. It turned out to be a very close match. In August 1996, Paul came over to Wales to donate his bone marrow. It was the first time they'd had a brother and sister in the transplant unit at the same time. Afterwards, Lisa remained in the unit. It wasn't quite full isolation, but not far off. She was allowed a maximum of two visitors a day and everyone had to gown-up to enter her shuttered room. It worked. Paul saved her life.

However, there was one huge side effect of the treatment that both of us had temporarily pushed to a far-off corner in our collective mind. Before the transfusion took place, part of the treatment involved flattening Lisa's own bone marrow. This meant she had to have a series of intense total body irradiation (TBI) therapy sessions. Such treatment would have a serious impact on her internal organs, including her ovaries, and that meant we wouldn't be able to have children. Forcing ourselves to consider all this so early on in our marriage, and bearing in mind how united we were in our desire to start a family, might well have been truly devastating.

But priorities change when faced with trauma. We put it to the back of our minds and were just glad that Paul had come up trumps and the transplant could go ahead. This meant Lisa stood a chance of full recovery. She had the transplant and was told that the following six weeks would be difficult. She might have infections or side effects. Luckily, she didn't have either to any serious degree.

In September 1996, Lisa was allowed out. She couldn't walk very far at all. She was very weak generally. But at least she was out. That was a huge relief for us both. It was a day we had feared might never come. On Lisa's first morning home, I woke to see that she wasn't in bed next to me. I was confused as to where she was and I panicked a little. Then I saw that she was standing by the bedroom window, which she had opened. I asked her what she was doing. She said that she hadn't been able to sleep and that she had stood at the window, listening to the birds. Her sensory perceptions were significantly heightened, and looking out over the fields to the front of our house was a visual and aural feast for her. It's the kind of thing you take for granted until you realize how fragile life is.

As that year came to an end, Lisa grew in strength. It's remarkable to me that, watching her through that eight-month period, I didn't see her lose confidence once. I never saw any doubt in her mind that she would recover. I think that determination and focus helped her to do so. A bleak and difficult time was made all that much easier by the fact that Lisa herself was so positive. She was an inspiration to many, and particularly to me.

SEVEN

Blair's Britain

IN THESE SOCIAL MEDIA DAYS of instant analysis in response to current events, it's so easy to fall back on all-encompassing words such as 'historical' or 'the best of all time' when we try to describe something that has taken place. We make those claims for so many events, not really knowing how they actually fit into the bigger picture of life, going back hundreds of years. 'Seminal' is another such word, whether it be a day or a moment or a year. But even with such timely caution, I think we can safely say that 1997 was indeed a seminal year.

Personally, of course, Lisa and I were delighted that we were able to begin that year together. That was more important than anything else. But so much else happened that year, in the wider world, that was to be of lasting influence on popular culture. For example, that's when the world first met the Teletubbies, saw the film *Titanic*, was able to buy the first *Harry Potter* book, and it's the last year the UK won Eurovision. On a completely different note, it was also the year when Lady Diana died, which sent shock waves around the world and led to years of debate as to the circumstances of her death, her legacy, and the whole future of the Royal family.

But for me, of course, the main public event that year was Tony Blair's landslide victory in the General Election. Labour gained 147 seats in Westminster, the Tories lost 171, including every seat they had in Wales and Scotland. It ended eighteen years of Tory rule in Westminster. Although, it must be said, that rule had been rather tenuous for many of the years before 1997. In that period, the Tories didn't have a clear majority, due to defections and lost by-elections. In fact, by 1997, they hadn't won a by-election since 1989. Tony Blair had been Labour leader for less than three years, following the untimely death of John Smith. But, in May 1997, he became Prime Minister. It was a fantastic time to be in the Labour Party. In fact, politics itself changed. People were ready for a big change at that point, and it felt like a wave of optimism was washing over the country in a way that hasn't happened since. The year 1997 was more than an electoral victory, it was a generational leap into modernity.

I was still a councillor at the time. The energy and enthusiasm the General Election landslide brought to

the party added a spring to the step, even for a councillor on the streets of Coity. But the biggest focus for me
happened when the devolution referendum of 1997 was
announced. The Labour Party, under Prime Minister
James Callaghan, had committed itself to devolution
in 1974 and then later announced a referendum on the
issue for 1979. But even though it was Labour policy,
there were many prominent Labour MPs in Wales who
were strongly against devolution. When the referendum
happened in 1979, devolution was defeated by 956,330
to 243,048 votes. The idea of devolution for Scotland
was also rejected by the Scottish people, albeit by a
far smaller margin. There were 1,230,937 in favour of
devolution there, and 1,153,502 against. Despite the
majority for it, the turnout was low, and the result
was less than the 40% of the electorate required by the
Scotland Act of 1978, so the Act was repealed. The fear
inside much of the Labour Party at this time was that
devolution represented the 'thin end of the wedge',
bringing with it the prospect of independence. For many
socialists, devolution seemed like a distraction.

The prospect of any form of home rule was anyway
kicked into the long grass when Callaghan lost to
Margaret Thatcher in the 1979 General Election. But
during eighteen long years of Tory rule, the idea of

devolving power became more and more mainstream within the Labour movement, culminating in a commitment in Tony Blair's 1997 manifesto. Riding on the crest of an electoral wave, the Blair government set up a devolution referendum for Wales and Scotland for that same year.

I was an instinctive supporter of devolution and didn't hesitate to set up and become Secretary of the Yes Campaign group in Bridgend and the neighbouring Ogmore. The sitting Labour MP in that constituency, Ray Powell, was an opponent of devolution, so that was a challenge from the off. Ray was a formidable operator and he didn't hold back on his views, which made for a challenging start to the campaign. Countering a simple 'No' message with nuanced arguments and explanations was as tough in 1997 as it would prove to be in 2016 over Brexit. But, gradually, we were hearing more and more people say that they were warming to the idea. There was a definite perception of momentum shifting as the campaign rolled on and people became more familiar with the idea.

On the paper on ballot day, which was 18 September, the public were asked to respond to two statements, printed in Welsh and English. We were asked to put a single cross next to one of those statements.

Parliament has decided to consult people in Wales on the
Government's proposals for a Welsh Assembly:
Mae'r Senedd wedi penderfynu ymgynghori pobl yng
Nghymru ar gynigion y Llywodraeth ar gyfer Cynulliad
i Gymru:

> **I agree there should be a Welsh Assembly**
> **Yr wyf yn cytuno y dylid cael Cynulliad i Gymru**

or

> **I do not agree there should be a Welsh Assembly**
> **Nid wyf yn cytuno y dylid cael Cynulliad i Gymru**

On the night of the results, as the first announce-
ments were being made, initially area after area were
declaring themselves against devolution for Wales. It
was fascinating but nerve-wracking to watch the evening
unfold. A pattern emerged. The more Labour the area,
the greater the Yes vote. This meant that the Valleys
were turning out in favour of devolution. This was a
change to the turn of events in 1979. But then there was
a run of authorities declaring a No majority again.

It was heading for a really close call. When all but
one of the results were in, there was nothing to choose
between the Yes and the No campaigns. All Welsh eyes
were on Carmarthenshire, the last county to declare. I
had heard earlier on during the day that Carmarthenshire had voted Yes. That's what happens in elections:

you hear the results before they are announced. What I didn't know, of course, was how that one result would play into the bigger picture. I then remember Huw Edwards on BBC News saying that they had heard that Carmarthenshire had voted Yes, and by a big majority. He then went on to suggest that that majority, if confirmed, would be enough to secure a Yes majority overall. That's what Carmarthenshire did, and that was indeed the nationwide result of their decision.

Carmarthenshire's Yes was enough to secure devolution by a majority of 6,721. Eleven unitary authorities in Wales voted in favour of devolution for the nation. Eleven voted against. But, of the majority of the 1,112,117 Welsh people who voted, 559,419 were in favour of devolution for Wales and 552,698 were against. A very slender majority, but a victory none the less.

If 'No' had won on that historic night – and that is a correct use of the word historic – then the very idea of Wales as a nation would have disappeared for many a generation. That would have been the second No vote in less than twenty years and no Westminster government would have considered giving us another chance at running even *some* of our own affairs again. Two No votes would have been a loud and clear message to London that Wales didn't want to know. It would have sent a message to the world as well, the message being that

Wales wasn't actually a proper country after all. It was just another region like any other. It would have affected our identity as a nation in the eyes of others. Maybe we would be reduced once again to having a meaningful separate identity only on the rugby and football pitches? And there's a question mark over whether we actually would've kept that in the longer term.

But it was a Yes. It was the start of a new Wales. 'Exciting times' is another well-worn cliché, but these really were. It was a stuttering start, but even so it unleashed a new confidence in the country. It changed the map of Wales, too. If you look at the devolution map of the nation it looks very much like the map of Norman Wales. It's an exercise that's worth trying. The Norman Lowlands and the Welsh Uplands of nearly a thousand years ago correspond almost exactly to devolution Wales 1997.

Now that we were to make our own decisions, and shape our own destiny, we needed people to step forward for election. I felt fortunate to be the one chosen to fight the first Assembly election for my hometown, Bridgend. It was a difficult selection to win, particularly given that one of the other candidates for selection was Brackla councillor Dave Sage. There were no hard feelings, though, and Dave was my agent in every election that I fought, and his humour and commitment were legendary. Sadly, Dave passed away far too young, in his fifties, after losing his wife, Anne, and suffering a run of bad health. We all miss him still.

Despite the buoyancy of the referendum result, it was not an easy time for the Labour Party. There was a clear division regarding the choice of who was to lead us. Alun Michael, as MP for Cardiff South and Penarth, was chosen, but many saw him as the choice of the London government. On 27 October 1998, he was chosen as Secretary of State for Wales. Two days later he was chosen as leader of the Labour Party in Wales. His predecessor in both roles, Ron Davies, was a popular figure and one who many in Wales thought was more suited for the job. Indeed, Ron had comfortably won the first leadership contest against Rhodri Morgan. Then, of course, came the infamous 'moment of madness' (the full details of which are unknown, but which started with him meeting a stranger on Clapham Common and ended with him being robbed at knifepoint) and Ron had to resign. What followed was a second contest for the leadership of Labour in Wales. Once again, Rhodri stood and won the votes of members convincingly. His opponent, Alun Michael, won hands down amongst the unions and MPs, and so the party's Electoral College delivered victory to Alun. Although Alun was always very committed to devolution personally, he was seen as Blair's man.

The Assembly election date was set for 6 May 1999.

It doesn't seem that long ago, really, but campaigning was decidedly old-fashioned compared to today. Back then it was all press releases (sent by fax), and there was little strategic direction in terms of the communities and households we would be targeting – nor in the messaging we would use. It came down to a lot of local nous and guesswork. Today, of course, technology allows campaign teams to focus much more forensically on certain areas and demographics, and with just the right content for each pair of eyes.

The Tory candidate in my constituency was a certain Alun Cairns. It certainly wasn't the last time our paths crossed, not least when he became Secretary of State for Wales. The election results weren't announced overnight in 1999. They were counted and verified, and it was the following morning when we had the declarations. They showed that I had won by a comfortable majority.

LABOUR	Carwyn Jones	9,321	37.2%
CONSERVATIVE	Alun Cairns	5,063	20.2%
PLAID CYMRU	Jeff R. Canning	4,919	19.7%
LIB DEMS	Rob O. Humphreys	3,910	15.6%
INDEPENDENT	Allan Jones	1,819	7.3%
Majority		4,258	17.0%
Turnout		25,032	41.6%

I was stunned, happy and scared all at once. Everything became a little 'real'. And as the results came in from other parts of the country, it was clear that the first-ever Assembly election had thrown up some serious surprises. The staunch Labour constituency of Islwyn was taken by the nationalist party, Plaid Cymru. The possibly even more staunchly Labour Rhondda Valley was also taken by Plaid Cymru. This sent shock waves through Wales and certainly through the Labour Party. When Plaid came very close to winning in Swansea, a city where it had no strong track record at all, we realized that we were likely to have a small majority in the new Assembly and we would have a political battle on our hands from the very start. In the end, with over a million people voting, Labour secured twenty-eight seats, Plaid Cymru seventeen, the Conservative Party nine, and the Lib Dems six.

Nobody had ever been an Assembly Member in Wales before, and so, with fifty-nine others, I began learning what that meant as we looked to make sense of this new political world. I took an office in the middle of Bridgend, above the hairdresser where my mother used to go. Political surgeries were certainly interesting in those early months. Very few people turned up for them, quite simply because they didn't really know what an Assembly Member (AM) was. On many nights no one turned up at all. Back then I would hold these surgeries in any one of twenty-one centres throughout the constituency. Today, I only hold them in my office in the town. And the simple reason for that is security. My constituency work in the early days was based on the working pattern of the area's MP, Win Griffiths, who I had campaigned for some years earlier. I soon realized how hard-working he was and realized too that I, as an AM, couldn't replicate the way he functioned as an MP. I found a system that worked for me in an Assembly context and developed that. In the Assembly itself, I took my place on the back benches of this newly constituted Government and felt a great pride in doing so.

But, however seminal 1997 was for Wales and for me politically, it didn't eradicate the problems that had faced Lisa and myself in 1996. Lisa might well have dealt with cancer, and I might well have been elected as an Assembly Member, but that didn't change the fact that we had been told we wouldn't be able to have our own children. No seismic political changes in Westminster or Cardiff would make us forget that fact. Discussions about children would dominate our lives from 1997 onwards. There were lots of private tears, especially during more difficult times. Around us it seemed like everyone was increasing the size of their own families, our closest friends and family members included. We responded with joy and congratulations, but inside our hearts were breaking. We knew it wasn't our God-given right to have children, but we somehow couldn't accept that parenthood would never be a part of who we were. How would we deal with this?

One thing was certain: we would explore every possible avenue. First, we tried a form of IVF called 'oocyte donation', which was an egg sharing scheme. That proved to be an emotional roller coaster, and a very expensive one. I understand that this and other forms of IVF have brought great results and much happiness to many couples, but for us it was an extremely difficult process that felt as if we were gambling with another roll of the dice each time we were thinking about whether to go ahead with another round. We tried three times towards the end of the decade, but to no avail. The emotional cost was enormous and eventually became too much to bear.

So we considered adoption. That was difficult for me to get my head around. It was a definite recognition that we wouldn't have children of our own. We had obviously confronted the possibility when first told of the effects of the radiation. But then there was always the possibility, a maybe, a who knows what might happen? Recognizing that IVF wasn't the path for us pushed those possibilities, those maybes, and the who knows, further and further into the distance.

My own personal response to this was based on my family circumstances. I was an only child. I was therefore the last in the line. The second chapter of this book shows the strength and depth of that line quite clearly. It's something that I am particularly conscious of and about which I have an innate awareness. Realizing that the biological line would end with me was an emotional and psychological struggle. It was something that I had to think through, time and time and time again. A gradual acceptance of that situation left me feeling as if a part of me had died. I felt this in my work as well. I did a lot of family law. In court cases related to this, I heard many stories of parents neglecting their children or using them as pawns in a bitter game. This used to infuriate me. Didn't they realize how lucky they were? I couldn't cope with men misusing a privilege that I might well not be able to enjoy myself. I asked to be taken off such cases in the end. The work–life balance had been well and truly upset.

But the priority for Lisa and me was to have children. We wanted to have that privilege and responsibility. We both knew what it was like to be a part of a contented and supportive family. We wanted to give others a chance to experience the same, and we decided that we would not let anything get in our way. First, though, we had to allow ourselves time to grieve for the children we would never have and convince ourselves not to feel guilty about this. It was only then that we could move on and consider adoption.

EIGHT

The Cabinet and Foot and Mouth

MY ARRIVAL AS a young and keen Assembly Member into the Senedd, as the debating chamber was called, led to my becoming a member of the Agriculture Committee. Being young and keen was probably the only real reason I was happy to be on such a committee, as I had no actual direct experience that qualified me for such a position. Any farmers in my family were back in my grandparents' day, or even before that. The mines, not the farms, were the architecture of my heritage. I certainly didn't enter politics with a view to being on the Agriculture Committee, but, much to my surprise, I really enjoyed it.

The first person that I'd met was John Griffiths, AM for Newport East. We became firm friends from the start. I've always admired John, because he came to politics the hard way. A young father, he'd worked in various jobs but had decided to qualify as a solicitor, which he did through night school and university while raising a young family. It made my route look easy. I also met Alun Pugh, AM for Clwyd West, on the first day. So close did we become that we were often referred to as the Three Musketeers, until Alun lost his seat in 2007.

That first year was tough because of the huge tensions within the Labour Group between Alun Michael's staunch supporters and those who felt Rhodri should have been First Secretary. I should make it clear that Rhodri did absolutely nothing to stoke those tensions. Things got worse, and eventually the threat of a no confidence vote by Plaid Cymru over the issue of Objective One match funding (This was EU funding that was made available to West Wales and the Valleys because of low GDP per head) led to Alun resigning. Rhodri then took over in February 2000. It was a sorry time for the new Labour Group and it was my first real introduction to the manoeuvrings and shifting sands of politics. There would be huddles of people talking quietly in corners and the discussions within the Labour Group were routinely leaked to the media. I have to say that I never really fitted into this kind of politicking and I often felt like I was the last one to know a piece of gossip that had been running through the corridors of the Assembly for weeks. It was just part of the place that didn't come naturally to me. Alun's mistake had been not to reach out sufficiently to those who hadn't supported him, but who were prepared to be loyal. It is an important part of leadership to be able to move on once a battle has been fought – but many in politics can't do it, and their circles of influence and trust become too small. Alun's decision not to reach out in that way was a hugely important lesson for me, and one I took on board in 2009 when I became First Minister.

ALUN LEFT the Assembly soon after and is now the Police and Crime Commissioner for South Wales. Over the years my respect and affection for him have grown. He took the job through loyalty to Tony Blair – he had been busily carving out a successful career in Parliament at the time – and I've never thought he had the recognition that he deserved. Alun also has one of the most singularly impressive work rates I've ever encountered in a politician: his energy is phenomenal.

At such an early stage in my political career, my mind hadn't drifted towards promotion. And so, when the call came, it was a surprise in more ways than one.

One Saturday in July 2000, Lisa and I had spent the evening in the living room with a welcome glass of wine each to unwind after a day of shopping when the phone rang quite late – at about 10.30 p.m. I thought about not answering it, but decided to do so, as it could be a family emergency, considering the lateness of the call. On the other end I heard the voice of Rhodri Morgan. He was at the time the First Secretary of the Assembly. The role was changed to First Minister in October of that year. Rhodri's message was short and to the point. In Welsh, he said, 'Right. I want you to take over from Christine as Agriculture Secretary on Monday.' As I said, surprising, short and to the point!

Christine Gwyther had been appointed Agriculture Minister by Alun Michael. But it was a decision that was heavily criticized, especially by Welsh farmers. She was a vegetarian, and the farmers thought that this would undermine her position in safeguarding their welfare, which was unfair on Chris, but that's the way it was seen. In politics you get a sense for the storms that will pass, and the others where you need to act, and the pressure on Chris just wasn't going away. Rhodri had spoken to her that Saturday afternoon to explain his decision and then rang me to replace her later that day. His phone conversation ended with him saying that he would pick me up the following Monday, so that we could go to the Royal Welsh Show together. If the phrase 'baptism of fire' hadn't already been invented, it could have been coined for this sort of start to a ministerial career. The Royal Welsh is the largest agricultural show of its kind in Europe. For most attendees it is great fun, and a way to catch up with friends and family – to buy and sell and showcase. A real celebration. For the Agriculture Minister, however, it is a real test of your mettle.

I was not supposed to tell anyone about the appointment, as the official announcement would be on that Monday morning. But I had to tell Lisa, obviously, and I rang my parents. They were in their caravan in New Quay that weekend and, when I rang, they were with people. So I had to tell them the news and at the same time ask them not to give the game away with their response in front of others. So, there we were. At thirty-three, I was a Cabinet Minister.

On the Monday, it all became very real. There were media interviews and many, many conversations with farmers, their representatives and their families. I was so glad the animals couldn't talk! It became clear quite quickly that it was a big advantage that I spoke Welsh. Many of the farmers felt far more at home speaking Welsh than English. I also knew that farmers loved an argument. So, in any meeting at which I was speaking, if I was shouted at during my speech, I responded robustly. It was obvious that they preferred this approach to any political posturing and spin. This went down really well and helped build a rapport that I was soon going to need.

Almost as soon as Christmas 2000 had gone, we were

hit by a massive crisis in the farming world, not only in parts of Wales but in other areas of the UK as well. In fact, it also eventually affected Ireland and some other areas of Europe. Foot and Mouth is a viral disease that affects cloven-hoofed animals, and the 2001 epidemic was widespread and disastrous for agriculture and tourism, and, as a result, for the economy. The problem with this outbreak was that it had started quite a while before anyone realized and therefore had been able to take a firm hold. It spread through Essex, Devon, Cornwall and Yorkshire, but by the time the disease was brought under control, Cumbria was the worst affected area.

I was in Northern Ireland visiting Lisa's family when I had a call to say that the disease had reached Wales. I had to fly back immediately. The first affected Welsh animals were in Anglesey and then in Powys. It's thought that it arrived in Monmouthshire via a pig farm in Gloucestershire. The problem for us was that while the movement of cattle was monitored and records were kept, this wasn't true of sheep and pigs. We had no idea where they might travel to and from. As a result, sheep were carrying the disease all over the place, undetected.

Because of the infection, it was not possible to sell any animal. There was a strict restriction on all animal movement. They could not go from farm to mart or from mart to mart. It also meant we couldn't export, which was a disaster for an industry that was, and is, dependent on the European market. This, of course, affected the prices significantly. There were also restrictions on people crossing agricultural land and many public footpaths were closed throughout Wales.

Such an epidemic, not previously experienced by most of us who had to deal with it, evidently caused concern and worry for farmers. Their livelihood was under serious threat. And, as is usually the case during such serious situations, the rumour mill began to churn out false information. It wasn't long before people were saying that they had heard the disease was spreading to such and such a place, and that, according to what someone said, this farm or the other had been closed down, and so on, and so on. Stories about how the disease spread were also circulating. One Welsh newspaper, the *Western Mail*, carried a letter that suggested that the disease was spread by helicopters spraying powder. Another story was about a farmer who had found a glass phial on his farm and felt that that was how the disease had reached him. It turned out the phial was a lightbulb! Others suggested that it was a deliberate attempt to decimate the agriculture industry. Such stories caused panic and uncertainty and hindered the process of dealing with the actual situation. In addition, people under pressure and full of fear will start believing things that meet their need to explain why what's happening is happening. Those things that are clung to aren't always based in truth or reality. To that end, I decided to hold press conferences every day. The intention was to present as many facts as we possibly could so that there were no gaps to be filled by gossip and rumour. Today, dealing with such a crisis in the age of social media would be an incredibly difficult thing to handle. At least we were able to head off most of the speculation and rumour before it got into mainstream thinking – Twitter could and would have seriously challenged our ability to do that.

But dealing with rumours wasn't the only challenge regarding the Assembly response to Foot and Mouth. Through a strange quirk of the devolution settlement, this wasn't actually a devolved issue. Animal disease generally was devolved, apart from Foot and Mouth. So we had no direct powers with which to respond. In law, therefore, the Ministry of Agriculture, Fisheries and Food (MAFF, as they were known) were in charge of dealing with the crisis. But the only staff they had in Wales were vets. So if they wanted to implement any strategy or policy in Wales, they had to use our civil servants. It was just bonkers that we had no control over such a serious situation. It highlighted the fundamental flaws in the weak form of devolution we had in Wales at that time. The people with the responsibility didn't have the resources, and the people with the resources didn't have the responsibility. Common sense prevailed, though, and we found a way of working together, without any serious friction between ourselves and Whitehall.

The reality of the situation that we faced was finding measures to control the disease and deal with the impact it had already had. Farmers faced bankruptcy. Rural businesses faced serious problems as a result of the measures put in place to deal with Foot and Mouth. We put up some financial aid to help alleviate this situation. Assembly Members as a whole would testify that they were inundated at that time by farmers visiting their surgeries, sharing concerns, asking for practical answers. It soon became apparent that AMs were, in effect, also offering a counselling service in many, many cases. The impact on farming families was devastating.

Rolling out an extensive vaccination programme was discussed. But such an approach had its limitations. Even if an animal was vaccinated, it would still be classed as having Foot and Mouth, with the same conditions imposed on it as every other infected animal, so it was a limited approach. It only served to stop the spread of the disease to other animals; it didn't make animals any healthier for the market. Those who advocated vaccination as the answer pointed to the Netherlands. 'That's what they do there,' was the comment. But the conditions in the two countries were entirely different. In the Netherlands, the animals were contained in fields. In Wales, the sheep especially were roaming over the hills and the mountains. The same answer wouldn't work for such differing situations. We did consider freezer ships at one point to store carcasses, but that proved impractical as well.

It became evident that the answer to dealing with the carcasses of the animals killed by the disease and the controlling of its spread was going to have to be a drastic and dramatic one. The carcasses had to be burned in one central point. Burning them farm by farm meant that the process just wasn't happening quickly enough. The disease was always a few days ahead of us. In the end, the vets told us that we had to cull healthy animals to create a cordon sanitaire and therefore stop the further spread of Foot and Mouth. This caused a great deal of anger among farmers, who couldn't understand why apparently healthy animals were being culled – the fact was that many of them had already contracted the disease but weren't yet showing symptoms.

I remember flying in a helicopter above one of these burning sites. It was horrific. There's no other word for it. Pyres of animal carcasses were obviously a very emotive image. They were a horrible sight that offended so many senses and sensibilities. But there was no other way of dealing with such a rampant epidemic. Every other available solution brought with it even more catastrophic possibilities. Choosing a site in which to burn the carcasses was a challenge, however. It had to be both accessible and remote. Mynydd Epynt, on the edge of the Brecon Beacon National Park, was chosen.

Thousands of acres of this mountain had been acquired by the Ministry of Defence at the outbreak of World War II in 1939. It was still in the hands of the MoD in 2001, as it is today, being one of the largest military training grounds in the UK. But there had to be public consultation with local people before we could actually action this. After all, this was a sensitive issue but also in a sensitive location. When the local families were asked to leave the mountain area in 1939 in order to make way for the military, they received no compensation. That perceived injustice was still real, all those years later, and any mass movement into the area had to be dealt with sensitively. I'd done this on Anglesey, where the Penhesgyn landfill site was needed to dispose of infected carcasses from the island. The adjacent farmers weren't happy, so I went to meet them. I remember the meeting well. The room was full to bursting. One man in a checked shirt, standing at the back, was particularly vocal and arguing quite forcefully. At the end of the meeting he came up to me and introduced himself – as an undercover policeman!

That reflected the strength of the protests that were happening. The protests were often dramatic and intense, and many protestors wore white overalls or lab coats with white masks. Quite often, apocalyptic language would be used. I was accused many a time of causing the rivers of Wales to run with blood.

Cattle and sheep were eventually transported to Mynydd Epynt to be disposed of. But the protests still kept on happening. People voiced their anger at having, as they understandably saw it, infection transported to their area. The way the process started in the early days didn't help this. It was rather ramshackle, with lorries arriving in no particular order or formation. Sometimes animals were transported to the location with blood seeping out of the lorries, despite clear instructions to the contrary. On other occasions the backs of the lorries were open and the carcasses could be clearly seen. Understandably, this did not help to quell any protest.

In the midst of the crisis, I was invited to take part in a Welsh-language *Question Time*-type programme, *Pawb a'i Farn* (*Everyone Has an Opinion*). It was held at Llandovery College. Security was so different in those days to what it's like now. When I arrived at the college, there was one policeman. But many, many protestors!

They surrounded my car and started to rock it to and fro. The policeman tried his best, but ended up getting completely overwhelmed and having his helmet knocked off. I had to leave at the end of the evening with a police escort. Sometime after Foot and Mouth had finished, I was invited to open the village hall in Trecastle, one of the hotbeds of the protests. Some of the people there had been at the Llandovery protest. Over a cup of tea after the official proceedings, I casually mentioned that I was surprised to have been invited to perform the ceremony that day, in light of the protesting they had done on the college grounds. 'Oh, that wasn't us, they were outsiders, they were. They'd come from somewhere else to join in with us. Who knows where they were from!'

The operation at Mynydd Epynt was soon plotted meticulously and properly, which took the sting out of many objections and helped calm the situation. But the concern escalated a little once again when it was announced that the army would be involved in running the process, though it soon calmed down again when the efficiency of the operation was seen. There's no doubt that, if it wasn't for Epynt, we wouldn't have dealt with the situation adequately.

The disease had largely disappeared from Wales by May 2001, but there was then a separate outbreak on Pen-y-Fan in the August. How it got there out of the blue, with no apparent connection to any other infected area, is a mystery to this day. In total, over six million cows and sheep were killed in the UK. The last known outbreak was in September 2001, in Cumbria. The UK Government downgraded the situation in November and the last cull was on New Year's Day 2002, in Northumberland. It had been a year of devastation, havoc and heartbreak for the farming community.

In addition to that, and the impact on agriculture and tourism, there were other broader effects of the disease. Events were cancelled, such as the British Rally Championships and the Cheltenham Festival, as well as hundreds of local fêtes and carnivals. Rugby's premier northern hemisphere competition, the Six Nations Championship, was also affected. The three games that Ireland were to play against the home nations in that competition in 2001 were postponed until later in the year. The General Election planned for that year was delayed by a month in order to stop the unnecessary flow of people travelling en masse to vote.

As with any crisis, not all the stories were doom and gloom. There was some discussion as to whether the pig that starred in the popular 1995 film *Babe* had been affected or not. Many were concerned for the well-being of this film star. But I'm glad to say that reports of his illness were greatly exaggerated.

Once the disease was dealt with, one thing that we secured immediately was the devolving of all future agricultural issues to the Welsh Assembly. So the responsibility for the Veterinary Service and Foot and Mouth was handed over to Cardiff. After that, the focus was on rebuilding Welsh farming and Welsh food – lamb in particular. That wouldn't be easy, as there was already stiff competition from New Zealand. But we had confidence in our produce. This was also the time when people started to be far more inquisitive as to where their food came from. There was a change in attitude without a doubt as a result of Foot and Mouth. People wanted more information before choosing what to buy. This, in turn, influenced the increasing emphasis on sourcing food more locally. Foot and Mouth caused a definite rethink.

This was true for farmers as well. Before Foot and Mouth, there was a certain animosity between agriculture and tourism, but the epidemic made it clear to everyone that they were both very much interdependent. Farmers became far less suspicious of tourism. Instead of talking in terms of agriculture and tourism, we started to emphasize the rural economy, which encompassed both, without distinction.

On a personal level, it helped a great deal that I lived in Bridgend. Just as it was not a coal mining town, it was also not a farming town. It allowed me a retreat from the intensity of the situation, which certainly helped me to deal with it. Back home, after everything had ended, it was time to reflect. About six months after unexpectedly being asked to be Agriculture Minister while sitting at home having a glass of wine, I was thrown into dealing with the biggest catastrophe the farming world had seen in the UK in nearly half a century. And this, of course, within an establishment that was brand new and relatively untested, so there were no obvious procedures or precedents. It was challenging. When it all ended, I knew that it would either make me or break me. It also gave me a lifelong respect for our farming communities in Wales, and the relationships I forged at this time long outlived my time as Agriculture Minister.

After the UK Government downscaled the Foot and Mouth epidemic, Lisa and I had some news of our own. The adoption process had borne fruit. That November, we were told they had found a little sixteen-month-old girl for us. She had huge brown eyes, she spoke a few words – not many – but she had a few. We were both absolutely overjoyed.

I remember so clearly those first tentative steps she took towards us. After that meeting, we were able to take her home with us. We were told by the adoption agency that if she slept well then she was feeling settled. This only took three days. She settled really quickly.

She had a birth name, of course, but we wanted to give her one of our own. We wanted a Welsh name and so we chose three – Seren Haf Catrin. Seren means star, which was quite an unusual choice at the time but is more common now. It's also the Welsh equivalent of Stella, my mother-in-law's name. Haf means summer, and we chose it because she was born in July. My mother's first name was Katherine, although everybody knew her by her second name, Janice, so the Welsh form Catrin was in honour of her and also, as Lisa is Catholic, we needed a saint's name too. The poor girl has quite a burden to carry!

Seren moved in with us and settled really well. We were obviously cultured parents, as we used to play Classic FM to her at night to help her sleep. Mention that to her now and she just rolls her eyes! I don't know if it was the music, but Seren never had any trouble getting off to sleep. She came to us a few weeks before Christmas, so our first family Christmas was soon upon us. That was really special and a big help in the process of the three of us settling with each other. I was a little unsure as to how my family would take to Seren. Not so much her as a person, but more the idea that we had adopted. Any fears turned out to be unfounded. We arrived at my parents' house and, as Lisa took Seren out of the pram, the door opened and they were welcomed like the return of the prodigal son. I put the pram in the garage and turned to see the front door had been closed. Obviously, their only son had been relegated to the back of the queue. For my grandmother, in particular, the arrival of Seren made her Christmas.

Having a child in the house did give me many, many practical challenges, as it does any new parent. My first major one was on that first Christmas. We had bought Seren a car, one she could sit in and propel with her feet. I decided that I would put it together after she'd gone to bed, just like any good father, but I couldn't fix the roof on to the damn thing. I struggled for hours, but couldn't for the life of me work out how to fix it. Lisa suggested I call my father, who was, of course, technically minded and an expert craftsman. But I refused. Eventually, Lisa persuaded me to ask my dad and he arrived later that night, and fixed the thing in less than thirty seconds. My reluctance to call him was a combination of refusing to admit I couldn't do it, and a new father's pride in wanting to do something for his child.

So there we were: Lisa and I as parents, at last. The whole issue of having children had dominated a good five years of our relationship, but there had never been any tension between Lisa and myself about it. We faced it together and dealt with it together. I never saw it as her challenge, but as *our* challenge, together. The cancer treatment that had put us in this situation was the same treatment that saved Lisa's life, and for that I could never be anything other than grateful. And with Seren's arrival, all of our other issues simply evaporated.

One day, we were walking up the street to my parents' house, with Seren in her buggy, and Lisa turned to me and asked, 'Do you ever wonder what our child would have looked like?' I instinctively turned to her, pointed to Seren in the buggy and said, 'That's what she looks like.' I wasn't trying to be contrived or to give the right answer. It's what came out of me as being the most natural thing in the world to say.

NINE

Of Government and Rainbows

WITH LABOUR HAVING no overall majority in the
first Assembly election, the party's grasp on the control
of government was very insecure. For the first year
Alun Michael was First Secretary, and initially he ran
a minority government. This proved to be challenging.
When Alun Michael left, replaced by Rhodri Morgan,
the need for stability resulted in a pact between Labour
and the Liberal Democrats. Lib Dem leader Mike
German was appointed to the newly created post of
Deputy Minister, as well as Economic Development
Minister. This happened in October 2000. Labour were
the majority party in the arrangement, but there would
be joint decisions on matters of governance, including
appointments of ministers. As with any coalition deal,
it put a few noses out of joint, Peter Law, Minister for
Local Government, being the most obvious example, as
he lost his ministerial job to make way for a Liberal.

Within only a few months this new working relationship was severely tested in the most unexpected way. In
May 2001, Mike German was embroiled in an expenses
dispute with his previous employers, the Welsh Joint
Education Committee. The WJEC claimed that there
were monies owed to them by Mike German through
use of their credit cards while he was away on European trips. When the calls for Mike to step aside started
to increase in number and volume, Rhodri Morgan
defended the Deputy Minister, saying that the charges
had no basis even when it was confirmed that the police
were investigating. Mike denied the charges from the
start, saying that making such allegations public was a
politically motivated action.

However, as the police investigation continued, it
became inevitable that he had to step aside until the
matter was resolved. His place as Deputy First Minister
was taken by Culture Minister Jenny Randerson. Rhodri
stated at the time of the suspension that he would accept
Mike back if he was cleared. The Queen addressed the
Assembly in June 2002, as part of her Jubilee Tour,
and no sooner had she left the building than Rhodri
announced that Mike German could be reinstated. The
police, he said, found that there was insufficient evidence
against him.

This was a difficult and rocky period for the Welsh

Government because, as much as anything, it was so new. We didn't need a scandal of whatever proportions within a year of starting, especially after such a hard-fought battle to establish the Assembly in the first place.

Mike's readmission led to Rhodri reshuffling the cabinet and Mike was put in rural affairs. Subsequently, I was moved to a new post, the wonderfully titled Minister for Open Government. I was, of course, a young AM in those days. Had I had any more experience under my belt, I would have told Rhodri, 'That's a daft title – it's almost like something from *Yes Minister*!' Basically, it meant dealing with freedom of information and equality – I had no problem with that at all – but I took over a department where one team was disjointed, to say the least. People were fighting for their own corner, refusing to gel as a team. It was very difficult, and dealing with the staff members actually took more of my time than the issues we were meant to be dealing with. It was really basic stuff: badly written letters, lack of information in briefings, back-stabbing and lack of discipline. Not really the kind of work that inspires you to get into politics, but it was illuminating in its own way about the ways government worked, or on occasion it didn't work.

As 2002 progressed, thoughts turned to the Assembly election that was to be held in 2003. I was selected again to be the candidate for Bridgend. When, after polling day, the election results were in, there was a clear distinction between my personal fortunes and the Labour Party's in general. The party had succeeded in consolidating its position following their inability to secure a clear majority in the first Assembly election. We had ridden many early storms, and the fruit of that was clearly seen in the 2003 election results, as the party gained more seats and all of our Assembly members increased their majorities – apart from me! I was once again up against Alun Cairns as the Conservative candidate. Bridgend Council at the time was very unpopular and Alun ran a very clever Assembly election campaign by attacking the council's record, not mine. This tactic succeeded in halving my majority. Bridgend is by no means a shoe-in for Labour. It has had a Conservative MP in the past and now has one again. When I saw how well everyone else had done in comparison, I was very down-hearted about everything. Halving your majority isn't the best result at any time, but having that happen when every colleague was increasing theirs made me despondent. But at least I had won.

LABOUR	Carwyn Jones	9,487	42.8	+5.6
CONSERVATIVE	Alun Cairns	7,066	31.9	+11.7
LIB DEMS	Cheryl A. Green	2,980	13.5	−2.2

PLAID CYMRU	Keith Parry	1,939	8.8	−10.9
UKIP	Tim C. Jenkins	677	3.1	N/A
Majority		2,421	10.9	−6.1
Turnout		22,113	35.4	−6.4

I took my place in a Labour Government that had increased its majority by winning two more seats. Plaid Cymru went backwards from their high watermark in 1999, and lost five seats. There was definitely a sense that, in 1999, many traditional Labour voters felt more inclined to vote for Plaid in what they saw as a 'Welsh election', but Plaid never capitalized on that early sway in their direction, and that momentum has drifted away ever since. They had been led into the 1999 election by Dafydd Wigley, a popular and well-known figure. Before long, however, he had been pushed out and they lost support as a result.

The Tories had gained two more seats and the Lib Dems stayed the same. In a sixty-seat chamber, Labour's tally of thirty seats was one short of a clear majority. To the delight of most of the Labour Group, Rhodri Morgan chose to go it alone and so his first Labour-only government was formed.

Rhodri called me in to ask me to renew my links with agriculture, but this time I was to take on environmental issues as well, along with town and country planning. It was a much wider brief and, more to the point, an unusual political step, because you don't normally go back to a department you've been in before. That caused me one very definite problem.

There are two farmers' unions in Wales. The National Farmers Union and the Farmers Union of Wales. The FUW was formed by a split from the NFU in 1955. The feeling among the Welsh farmers that wanted to leave the NFU back then was that the specific needs of Welsh hill farmers were being ignored by a lowland establishment of big farms in England. Before the 2003 election, there had been quite a lot of talk about merging the two unions once again. I had occasion to comment on this idea and I said that I thought it was a good one. The two should merge, I said, and be more effective together as a result. I said this in full confidence that I would not be going back to being a minister with responsibility for farming. How wrong I was! It was with fear and trepidation that I accepted the new responsibility for rural affairs. Thankfully, the expected storm didn't happen and it would appear very few people remembered what I had said about merging the unions. I could carry on quietly. But two valuable political lessons had been learned. One, be careful what you say during a campaign, and two, be thankful that not everyone pays attention.

One of the early projects we started at that time was the Wales Coast Path. The plan was to have a dedicated pathway all around the Welsh coast. We worked in conjunction with the then Countryside Commission for Wales, the relevant local authorities and two national parks. Such a massive project wasn't going to happen overnight. Rhodri Morgan unveiled the first plans in 2006 with the opening of the path around the Isle of Anglesey. The full path was opened in May 2012. Wales was the first country in the world to open a designated path around its coastline.

The planning aspect of my department wasn't as seemingly straightforward as the other aspects of the work – far from it. I saw a complete mix of planning applications, ranging from the sublime to the ridiculous. One authority that always gave me planning headaches was Ceredigion, on the west coast of Wales. I saw some strange applications coming from there. I remember them wanting to give planning permission for something because the person behind it was a well-liked figure in the local community. I saw a lot of that. It was certainly a department where you came across people who were angry or passionate about the application they were championing, and quite often they were both angry and passionate in equal measure. In such circumstances, the only way through it was to look at the facts alone. Even then, people were at a loss to see how you had come to your decision and why you couldn't see things their way. But they were good years politically for me.

As 2003 CAME TO an end, Lisa and I had started to talk about adopting a second child. Soon after Christmas that year we were contacted by the adoption agency to say that they had found a child they thought suited us. It was a boy this time, who was also sixteen months old when we first met him, as Seren had been. A beautiful, blond, blue-eyed, bouncing boy with a very wheezy chest. We were thrilled. Here was a boy who would carry on my family name.

He had been on inhalers for most of his short life and didn't settle as well as Seren did. He had trouble sleeping at night too and didn't have a full night's sleep until he was about nine years old. Within a week of arriving at our home, he was in hospital with what we thought was very bad asthma. It was, in fact, stress and anxiety related. Those early days were obviously a major adjustment for him.

Seren was given a Welsh name, so in the spirit of international harmony, the boy was to have an Irish name. Ruari Wyn James: the second name was after my father and the third after one great-grandfather. I know that three names seems a bit much, but Lisa insisted that our children had to have a saint's name, in keeping with Catholic tradition. We soon added an extra letter so that Ruari became Ruairí, with a 'fada' over the last í. All to do with slender and broad vowels in the Irish language, apparently. We now had two children, which was another major adjustment for us initially, but one which meant so much to us.

It was so different to have a boy in the house. He wanted to take everything apart and it was difficult keeping up with him. I caught him once trying to cut through an electric cable with scissors – on his sister's insistence – so they got on well enough! On holiday in Brittany one year, I was in the play area with him, and I turned round and he had gone. Vanished! I couldn't find him anywhere and my blood absolutely ran cold. Luckily, one of the staff soon turned up holding his hand and leading him back to me. We had to keep our eyes on him all the time. I felt a complete and utter failure, used as I had been to a daughter who never left my side.

When Ruairí arrived, Lisa and I discussed adopting a third child in due course. Those discussions came to a head in 2007. I turned forty in the March of that year. But it was also the year of another Assembly election, and it was going to be a key one. Tony Blair was still Prime Minister but coming to the end of his popularity.

In 2003, he had experienced a boost in support, after the initial 1997 success – the 'Baghdad Bounce', as Rhodri Morgan called it. But then, after 2003, when more and more information about Iraq came to the surface, he wasn't quite so popular by any means. The opinion polls certainly reflected that as the election drew nearer.

When the results were declared, there was a direct reversal of 2003. I increased my majority, not by much, but it was an increase. The Labour Party, however, lost seats. We ended up with twenty-six seats, four fewer than in 2003. Plaid increased their number by three and the Tories by one. The Lib Dems stayed the same at six, as had been the case since the first Assembly election.

LABOUR	Carwyn Jones	9,889	40.3	−2.5
CONSERVATIVE	Emma L. Greenow	7,333	29.9	−2.0
LIB DEMS	Paul Warren	3,730	15.2	+1.7
PLAID CYMRU	Nick H. Thomas	3,600	14.7	+5.9
Majority		2,556	10.4	−0.5
Turnout		24,552	41.2	+5.8

Labour was still the largest single group, though. But once again we didn't have a working majority. This time, with a reduced majority, there was a need to discuss coalitions. Many options were discussed. A rainbow coalition was the foremost of those options, and talks between the Conservatives, Lib Dems and Plaid, excluding Labour, went very well at the start. They got to the point of deciding on who would have various responsibilities, with Plaid Cymru leader Ieuan Wyn Jones chosen as First Minister. At that point, we in the Labour Party were going to be the opposition and we were starting to seriously prepare for such an eventuality.

I was with Rhodri Morgan in Llandudno at the Wales TUC conference during these rainbow discussions. We were discussing how we would run the party in opposition, as we felt at that point it was as good as a done deal. In fact, *The Times* had already written a profile of Ieuan Wyn Jones as the likely next First Minister. Then the ever-democratic Lib Dems decided that they needed to put the idea before their own National Council, who failed to support it. So there was deadlock on the rainbow coalition. I heard the news when I went downstairs for breakfast at the Llandudno B&B that Rhodri and I were staying in. In those days of no social media, I asked him if there was any news on the coalition. 'Yes,' he said nonchalantly, 'it's been rejected.' I couldn't believe he was so matter-of-fact about such a big news story. But that was Rhodri.

So talks then turned to a Labour and Plaid Cymru

coalition government. Plaid said that working towards increased devolved powers for the Assembly was a condition of forming such a coalition. This was going to be a massive step for both parties and not one to underestimate. Historically, both parties were rivals, often bitter rivals in many parts of Wales. Given some of the shared ambitions the parties hold, it is often hard to grasp the animosity between the two. Fights in council chambers were not uncommon in the 1970s. Family members who were in one party wouldn't talk to family members in the other. If you were in one party, you wouldn't greet a member of the other party if you were passing him or her in the street and, if you did, you'd be heavily criticized by your own. This was particularly true in the 60s and 70s, but such a legacy was still in the blood decades later.

It's fair to say that within the Labour Party there was a natural suspicion of adopting a distinct Welsh identity, in case it would be seen as a drift towards nationalism or, at least, the thin edge of it. The charge of being a 'crypto-nat' was one used fairly liberally towards those of us in the vanguard of the pro-devolution section of the party. When I suggested in a 2003 pamphlet that we called ourselves Welsh Labour, there was a significant number within our party in Wales who didn't approve of that. That pamphlet, 'The Future of Welsh Labour', contains numerous suggestions that have since happened and are regarded as uncontroversial, such as law-making and revenue-raising powers. They were pretty controversial at the time, though. The argument, for some, was that it sounded as if it was only for Welsh speakers. Others thought that it sounded too much like a nationalistic statement, a desire to break free. There was, back then, a real aversion to being identified as being 'too Welsh', because of perceived associations with nationalism.

There were still some Labour MPs, at the time of the coalition talks in 2007, who were dead against any talks with Plaid Cymru. 'Go it alone!' they said, even though they wouldn't be the ones to have to manage four years in government, if we did. But Rhodri didn't see it that way. With the formation of the Assembly, a new forum for political debate had been created. There was an opportunity now to do things differently and move on from the bitter past. Among the people of Wales, attitudes had changed sufficiently over the first years of that new Assembly for us to get to the point, in 2007, where Labour and Plaid leaders could, and did, sit around the table and talk of governing Wales together.

But such a decision couldn't be taken exclusively within the leadership of both parties. The broader membership needed to be consulted. So a conference was arranged for the Labour Party to hear the views of its members. It was held in what was then the CIA venue in Cardiff. It was a very difficult event. All the bitterness mentioned earlier had not dissolved completely, and it surfaced in that meeting. Neil Kinnock spoke and was very strongly against any coalition with Plaid, as were two other MPs, Don Touhig and Paul Murphy. Their seniority carried a lot of weight.

A woman then stood up to speak. She was a teenager and spoke very eloquently. At one point she started to point at the three MPs who had spoken against the proposed coalition. We were taken aback at this, as the three could be regarded as grandees of the party. They were sat next to each other in the front and she made it very clear that she knew where they were and aimed her comments directly at them. I wondered who this person was and was told it was Estelle Hart, daughter of Edwina, the Assembly member for Gower since 1999, who would be Minister for Health and Social Services in the Assembly after the 2007 election. When her daughter spoke, I could hear the family resemblance, and I've teased Edwina about it many a time.

That meeting was very divisive. But those of us who were comfortable with forming a coalition with Plaid Cymru knew the meeting would end with the proposal being passed, as it was backed by the unions. Even so, it took its toll on everyone involved. Rhodri Morgan in particular paid a high price for his role in such seismic political shifts, as he suffered a heart attack not long after. He was rushed to hospital just in time and he thankfully survived. That meant a major shift for Rhodri as well. He became an evangelist for healthy eating. Sadly, despite this, he was taken from us ten years later.

In the beginning, when the Assembly was established, it was, in effect, an administrative body with very little power. As the Foot and Mouth story showed, Wales had some powers over some aspects of government departmental work, but not all. We were responsible for farming, but not Foot and Mouth. We had a little bit of this, but not that; we had some of the other, but not all of it. It made very little sense. That changed in 2006 with the passing of the Government of Wales Act, which increased our powers in the Assembly. This created a separate executive (Welsh Assembly Government) and legislature (the Assembly itself), with the former answerable to the latter. We now looked more like Westminster than a council. That's when we actually became more of a proper government, with the Welsh Assembly Government becoming a legal entity. That was probably overlooked by many people in Wales, but it was a big step ahead for the nation.

The system was put in place as a result of the Act, whereby we could amend Acts of Parliament, which we couldn't do before. We also now had clearly defined areas – or 'fields', as they're called – that were our responsibility.

I think it's worth listing the fields we became responsible for after 2006, just to emphasize quite what a shift had taken place. If nothing else, it will create the picture of the kind of Assembly I would become responsible for as First Minister. So here's the list: agriculture, fisheries, forestry and rural development; ancient monuments and historic buildings; culture; economic development; education and training; environment; fire and rescue services and promotion of fire safety; food; health and health services; housing; local government; highways and transport; public administration; the National Assembly for Wales; social welfare; sport and recreation; tourism; town and country planning; water and flood defence; and the Welsh language.

Quite a list. And one I'm sure that many in Wales still don't fully appreciate. That last field on the list – the Welsh language – might seem to be an obvious addition, but its inclusion in matters for which the Assembly had law-making responsibility was a first in 2006. Up until then, we had the incongruous situation where we couldn't pass major laws affecting our own language

The system was a cumbersome one, though. The Assembly had to request that Westminster grant power to the Assembly to amend an Act of Parliament. After due and lengthy deliberation, Parliament would grant a Legislative Consent Order. Then we would start the process of passing a Measure, which looked like, but wasn't quite, an Act. Needless to say, it took years to get anything done, while the Scots just got on with things.

This was the nature of the Assembly by the time of the 2007 election. When the coalition talks began after that election, Plaid Cymru were arguing that the 2006 Act didn't go far enough, just as they had done when it was passed. They wanted more powers for Wales, more akin to self-governance, but this was not enough of a stumbling block for Rhodri Morgan and the Labour Party to refuse a coalition arrangement. Labour and Plaid therefore formed the next government in the Assembly, with Plaid leader Ieuan Wyn Jones becoming Deputy First Minister.

The centre of political gravity had certainly shifted. The Government of Wales Act had seen it shift from Westminster to Cardiff. And in Cardiff, the Labour and Plaid Cymru coalition shifted it even further. What was at one time anathema was now up and running and would end up working very well.

TEN

First Minister, Melanoma and Climate Change

WHILE THE coalition talks were taking place, the governance of Wales had to continue. Rhodri Morgan had to form a cabinet with the knowledge that some posts would, quite quickly, have to be filled by Assembly Members from Plaid Cymru if the coalition was formed. Consequently, there were some strange departmental permutations while he waited for the political dust to settle. I was given the education, culture and the Welsh language brief, which usually covers a number of different departments. I did that job for a whole seven weeks. I used to say that I met teachers once, told them what they wanted to hear, and then let them get on with it!

As soon as the coalition was made official, there came the inevitable changes to shape the new Government. There was a suggestion that I should be appointed Counsel General, a kind of equivalent to the Attorney

General, the Government's legal adviser. It was a new job, but I had no desire to do it. I hadn't been practising law for years and I had no experience of devolved law. Thankfully, that suggestion didn't come to pass. Well, not quite as originally intended, anyway. Rhodri then offered me the role of Minister for Democratic Renewal. Another *Yes Minister* job title, I thought to myself. I had to ask Rhodri for an explanation of what that actually meant. It was, he said, to include Counsel General responsibilities and other related ones as well, which, up to that point, had come under other departments. I would also be responsible for government business in the Assembly. I knew enough about the constitution to know that if you were Counsel General then you couldn't have any other ministerial responsibilities that involved exercising ministerial functions, so I couldn't actually be a minister with executive power. As the discussions continued, it became clear that what Rhodri had in mind was something very close to the role of Leader of the House in the Commons. There were more challenges here: there had never been such a role in the Assembly at that time, and, secondly, Rhodri still wanted me to be Counsel General. So in the classic tradition of political compromise, he united the two roles and I became Counsel General and Leader of the House. I was the first to fill both roles.

The coalition talks were finalized and formalized and a Labour/Plaid coalition government was established to govern Wales. We had both Plaid and Labour ministers. It worked very well on the whole. It's fair to say that the main difficulties for our working relationship came from some of those in Westminster putting pressure on us. It was a big departure for the Labour MPs to see Plaid in government, and every time they secured a bit of decent coverage there was sniping that they were 'running rings around us in government'. Elements outside the Assembly group sometimes took things into their own hands. Ieuan Wyn Jones in particular came under a bit of fire. We were then in the position of facing accusations from Plaid AMs or political reporters of 'You said such and such . . .', meaning Labour as a whole, but Welsh Labour saying 'Well, actually, no, that came from London, we didn't say that . . .' It was an interesting and significant change in dynamic. But any such issues were always dealt with in-house. Through this, a specifically Welsh approach was being forged.

WHILE THE two parties were getting better acquainted in government, so were our two children at home. And with Seren and Ruairí settling in with us and with each other, we started to think about adopting a third child. We arranged a family holiday in Anglesey in August of 2005. The evening before we were due to leave, Lisa came downstairs looking ashen. She sat on a chair in the living room and said that she had a pain in her chest and down her left arm. I suggested calling for an ambulance. She refused, but it got to the point where I had to take her down to the hospital myself. My parents were away, so the next-door neighbours came in to look after the children. She was kept in hospital for several days. I went to see her on her second day and Berna, Lisa's elder sister, was with her. A few days later, her younger sister, Rebecca, took over. In light of Lisa's previous health issues, her sisters were as distressed as I was with the thought of her in hospital again.

The symptoms might well be different, but the sound of the alarm bells was just the same. The symptoms were obviously those of having had a heart attack. As a consequence of the cancer treatment Lisa had undergone, her heart had been another one of the organs affected. There were no other obvious risk factors in Lisa's diet or lifestyle that suggested heart issues were possible, and she was only thirty-eight. She was transferred to Morriston Hospital's cardiac unit, where it was confirmed that she hadn't had a heart attack, but instead had experienced heart failure: dilated cardiomyopathy. Not only that, we were told that it was progressive and that she would need a heart transplant at some point in the future. The only potential lifeline offered to us was a drug that could control the condition and prolong the need for a transplant. We took that option.

The day-to-day reality for us fell back into facing the possibility that Lisa had a life-threatening illness. But this time with two children in the family. The emotional stakes were higher, more complicated, more devastating. We might well have been there before, but, in another way, it was a completely new situation for us to face. We didn't have to think of any implications for any children following Lisa's cancer diagnosis. Now we did. It concentrated the mind and the heart in an intense way. It was tough.

That was in 2005. Fifteen years on, her condition is regulated and all the relevant indicators are normal. A transplant isn't on the agenda. Once again, medicine had intervened in deciding the nature of our family. It led us to a contented acceptance of being a husband, wife and two-child family. We were also very fortunate to have help from a great childminder, Stacey Wyatt-Williams, who's a mum herself now. She was invaluable to us.

Before the election in 2007, Rhodri Morgan made it clear that he was going to stand down as leader of the Labour Party very soon. He would not be First Minister, either. When I heard this, I would be lying if

I said that I didn't consider going for the job. But a lot of work needed to be done in the meantime. Lisa's illness certainly gave me pause for thought – the considerations certainly weren't exclusively political. But, by the time Rhodri said definitely that he would be standing down at the end of 2009, I had got to the point where I was ready to go for it, if I could secure the necessary encouragement and support. In the process of working out if that support was there or not, I had a meeting with Cathy Owens in the Café Rouge in Cardiff Bay. I'd known Cathy since she had been one of Rhodri's Special Advisers. We drew up a list of AMs and MPs and who they were most likely to support in the leadership race. When that work was completed, we left and then soon realized that we had left the list in the café! We dashed back there in fear that it had been leaked in the time that had elapsed since we'd left it there. Fortunately, there was no one with any great interest in the inner workings of Welsh Labour working in the café, otherwise my forward planning might have been undone at the first very informal hurdle.

Before my thoughts could turn fully to the future, however, there was a major issue to deal with in Bridgend. At the start of 2008 there had been a sudden jump in teenage suicides in the county. Following normal procedure, the computer of one victim was taken by the police.

Somehow, a journalist in London got hold of this and it started a media firestorm about Bridgend. There was talk of suicide pacts and cults. Journalists harassed students coming out of the local college. Doors were knocked at the homes of grieving parents. The press were like hyenas.

To top it off, much of the reporting was stained with the prejudices of London-based journalists about Wales. Bridgend was a 'depressed seaside mining town with high unemployment'. The only part of that description that's correct is that it's a town. They claimed the young people who died by suicide had all known each other because Bridgend was a small place. Actually, the young people were from Bridgend County, some of them living miles apart, and the population is 130,000.

It made things far worse, and I have no doubt that the terrible reporting caused even more pain for the families. It was irresponsible journalism at its worst. As is so often the case, I'm glad to say that the Welsh media didn't join in the frenzy. Generally, it seems that the closer you are to a story, the more respect you have for the people involved. It was a lesson that illustrated the damage that inaccurate and sensationalist journalism can do.

*

As THINGS developed on the leadership front, I needed to put together a campaign team. I appointed Leighton Andrews as my campaign manager. He was very active and full of ideas. Sometimes these were a bit of a stretch regarding what might be acceptable in an internal campaign, which meant that we often had to thrash out a compromise. On one occasion he simply put the phone down on me when I was exasperating him. Leighton wouldn't exactly be on my Christmas card list these days, but he was a good campaign manager and we made a good team. The most important skill in politics, they say, is the ability to count – and the single most important task in any leadership campaign is making sure you're on the ballot paper. In this contest that meant securing the backing of at least six fellow Labour AMs. Edwina Hart had ten, I had nine, and Huw Lewis had seven. Others had dipped their toes into the contest, with Jane Hutt and even Leighton himself thinking about going for it at an earlier stage, but in the end it was just the three of us going on to the next stage of the leadership contest proper.

Once it started in earnest, the leadership battle was a tough slog and all three of us clearly wanted to win – none of us was there to make up the numbers. Even so, I will always be glad that the contest was fought in the best spirit. That is not something you could say about previous leadership contests in Wales, and the bad feeling of bitter campaigns lingers on after the contest has long since finished. As it was, this was a competition that made the politics at the time, and in the future, a good deal easier. And, as it turned out, it made my own personal life a lot easier as well.

I had to travel the length and breadth of Wales to speak at campaign meetings. I remember one day in particular when I had to speak at Connah's Quay in North Wales in the morning and then be in Newport in South Wales by the afternoon. I was shattered, coming out of that second meeting and wondering what on earth we were doing. But it just had to be done. Campaigns are about staying power, just as much as they are about strategy and messaging. You have to keep going.

There was one event in North-East Wales that we did miss, however, and very lucky we were too. Local AM Carl Sargeant was organizing my campaign in North Wales and had arranged lots of fund-raising events locally. We were on the way to another of these, this time in an Indian restaurant – not an unusual location for a Labour Party fund-raiser – but, as we approached, we got an urgent call from Carl, saying, in his own inimitable style, for us not to go there, as it had just been raided by the Border Agency!

The length of campaigns means you get to consider pretty much every idea under the sun. At one point, the campaign manager, Leighton Andrews, suggested a change of tactic, telling me that I should be more on the attack against the other candidates. I really didn't think that this was the best approach, because, after all, we were in the same party. He suggested that I needed to do so in order to show that I had the 'balls' to be First Minister. We agreed to differ on that one. I managed to get the support of most of the MPs, which was a big boost. Union support was also crucial, of course. Unison had decided not to back anyone and Unite supported Edwina Hart. So, without the backing of two large unions, it was going to be a difficult battle.

DESPITE ALL of this, I felt confident that I could win the support of most of the AMs and MPs in the final week, and things were going very well with the membership. The unions were still difficult to call. The betting companies were, of course, showing the odds for each candidate and, in the last two or three days of the campaign, for some reason, my odds went through the floor. Quite possibly the result of some overeager briefing by some of the other campaigns.

When it came to it, the results were announced on

1 December 2009 in the Millennium Centre, Cardiff Bay. It had been a tough year of campaigning but also a tough year personally for my family; in March we had discovered that my mother was terminally ill. She had been diagnosed with melanoma two years earlier and it had been dealt with successfully, or so we thought. But she had discovered a lump under her arm, and hospital tests confirmed that it was cancer and that it had spread. By December, my mother was very ill and in the Bwthyn Hospice in Bridgend. There were no prospects for a recovery. She was usually heavily sedated on morphine, but on the day of the results, the staff at the hospice brought her round so that she could watch on TV.

As I walked from Tŷ Hywel, the Assembly head-quarters, to the Millennium Centre, my mother was very much on my mind. I remember a voice coming into my head on that walk, asking, 'Would you give all this up if it would make your mother well again?' It was a very vivid question, quite loud in my mind. The answer, of course, was yes, I would, while at the same time realizing that, no matter how much I wished I could make that switch, it wasn't in my gift.

I walked into the centre with two speeches in my pocket. One was a full side of A4, the other was half a side of A4. The candidates were gathered together first to be told the results before they were announced publicly. I sat there with Mick Antoniw (my campaign treasurer). I expected the party secretary, Chris Roberts, to announce the results in some time-honoured order, with maybe a speech beforehand, but he just came up to us and said, 'On the first ballot, Carwyn has an overall majority.' That was it. So, I knew I had won. We were then led into the room where everyone else was, so that the official announcement could be made. Leighton Andrews, my campaign manager, was in there and, as he looked at me, I mouthed the words 'first ballot'. He misread my wording and thought I had said 'fucking lost'! Another member of my team saw me take a speech out of my pocket and open it out. But I only opened it out halfway and he thought that I was preparing to read the shorter of my two speeches, the one accepting defeat graciously. I then opened the page out fully and he realized that I had won.

The official announcement was made, confirming the results. I had 52% of the votes, Edwina Hart had 29.2% and Huw Lewis had 18.8%. There was no need for a second ballot because my majority in the first was sufficient. I had a congratulatory phone call from Labour leader Gordon Brown and then I did the rounds of media interviews. Some twenty miles away, in the hospice, my mother saw the announcement on television and the staff gave her a glass of champagne to celebrate.

Rhodri Morgan was officially standing down a few days later, so I had nearly a week of overlap with him before he retired. By the time of the swearing-in ceremony, my mother was in a coma. My father, Lisa, Seren and Ruairí came to the Assembly and saw me take my place as First Minister. My grandmother, who was staying with us at the time to be near my mother, was fully aware of what had happened, and was suitably delighted. At ninety-five, however, she was unable to come to the Assembly that day. But my mother never saw the ceremony, sadly, nor did she know anything about it.

There was plenty of work to do in those first few days as First Minister. First things first, I had a team to choose. But before I could even finalize that, I had to go to a climate change conference in Copenhagen. That was very much a high-profile topic in Wales even then, and my presence at the conference was seen as essential. I had a chat with my father when I realized that the conference was on the agenda. I said that I was happy not to go to Denmark, because of my mother's illness. We discussed this quite a bit and my father said in the end that it was important for me to go. As far as my mother was concerned, he said, there's nothing I or anyone else could do now anyway. That my mother would certainly want me to go. So I went. Plans were made for me to go there by train, as that was the most environmentally friendly way. But because of my mother's illness, I decided to go by plane, so that I would be away for a much shorter time. We stayed in a hotel in Malmö, Sweden.

On 15 December I was sharing the stage with the Premier of Quebec and Alex Salmond, the Scottish First Minister. At the end of the session I went outside and turned my phone back on. I saw two missed calls, one from my father and one from my wife. I knew why they had called. I rang Lisa first and she confirmed that my mother had passed away. I rang my father, who was understandably upset, but fairly composed at the time. I then rang my grandmother. She was absolutely inconsolable. She had lost another daughter and she was screaming down the phone. I flew back that day and was home by the evening to be with my family. The funeral was two days before Christmas, which added a certain poignancy to an already difficult time. The children were nine and seven and not really fully able to understand what was going on, especially as it was their first experience of a family bereavement.

I've never really forgiven myself for going to Copenhagen. As much as I know that there really wasn't anything I could do for my mother, it still eats away at me that I went, and that I wasn't there for my mother at the end. I will always regard that time as bitter-sweet. I may have achieved the top political office in Wales, but I had lost my mother. I can never really think about that time without both moments coming to mind.

ELEVEN

An Old Nation Comes of Age

IN PUTTING TOGETHER my first Cabinet, I knew that I didn't want to appoint only from among those who supported me. That would have been a bad move and very divisive, and I'd be repeating the mistake I'd watched Alun Michael make some years before. The leadership contest might well have been a relatively harmonious one, but there was still the need to unite the party and to set a clear path forward. You can't afford to create a situation that leads to simmering problems, especially within a small group. Of course it is expected that you'll repay the loyalty of those who've backed you along the way, but you should also include those who have not always seen eye to eye with you.

We were still in coalition with Plaid Cymru, and their Cabinet members would be staying. As well as their leader, Ieuan Wyn Jones, who was Deputy First

Minister and Minister for Economy and Transport, the party also had Alun Ffred Jones (heritage), Elin Jones (rural affairs) and Jocelyn Davies (housing and regeneration) in the Cabinet. That somewhat reduced the scope of the positions I had to fill from the Labour ranks.

My team, I decided, would include the two candidates who stood against me. Edwina Hart was Minister for Health and Social Services, her first Cabinet responsibility. Huw Lewis was Deputy Minister for Children. Huw had approached me about a week before the leadership result was announced to say that he thought that I was going to win, and, if that was the case, he wasn't keen on having a deputy minister role as he had been a deputy minister already. He said that he would rather not be in the Government. I had to be honest with him and I told him that there wasn't an obvious ministerial job for him in the new Cabinet, but that if he took the deputy minister role I was offering him, I promised that he would be a minister in the next cabinet in 2011, if I was still First Minister. He agreed, took the brief and I kept my word to him in 2011.

My campaign manager, Leighton Andrews, was given the children, education and lifelong learning brief. The other responsibilities were shared out among AMs who'd had previous ministerial responsibilities – such as Jane Hutt, Minister for Business and Budget

– and those who hadn't – such as Carl Sargeant, who was given the social justice and local government brief.

But it wasn't a process I was able to go through without having a big dilemma. Brian Gibbons had been Minister for Health for some years previously and he had been a loyal supporter of mine. He was also a very high-profile character and was extremely popular. But whichever way I juggled the departments and the individuals needed to fill them, I couldn't find room for Brian. I felt lousy about that, I must say, and lost sleep over it. Then, out of the blue, Brian rang me up to say that he had had a great time in government but that he didn't want to continue and there was no need for me to worry if there was no room for him in my new Cabinet. That was very generous of him and it lifted a huge weight from my shoulders. I've always found Cabinet reshuffles to be extremely difficult, and they have been from day one.

The role of Chief Whip was an interesting one to fill. I had someone in mind: Janice Gregory, the daughter of Ray Powell, the MP for Ogmore from 1979 until his death in 2001. Ironically, he was one of those Labour MPs who was opposed to devolution. But I knew that his daughter would be an ideal Chief Whip. She's one of the nicest people you could meet, but with a very strong character. She once had to deal with a party member who was refusing to toe the party line on an issue, and when rational debate had come to an end, she just turned to him and said, 'Listen, if you don't vote with us, I'll have your balls for earrings!' Just what you want in a Chief Whip! We had a conversation before I was announced as First Minister, in an informal gathering of AMs. Talk turned to potential Cabinet members, should I be successful in my campaign. Janice, who was a strong supporter of one of my rivals, Edwina Hart, said, 'Well, there'll definitely be no room for me, will there?' I didn't respond, because I knew the way I was thinking at the time.

When the day came to tell people what their new responsibilities were, I asked Janice to come to see me. She was reluctant at first, saying that she needed to know why before she decided to come to Cardiff to see me. She eventually turned up and I told her I wanted her to be Chief Whip. She played it really cool, saying that she very much enjoyed being chair of a committee and wasn't sure if she wanted to change that. Then she broke into a broad smile and accepted, laughing as she did so. She really didn't see that one coming. It was probably the only time for the next eight to nine years that I knew something before Janice did.

So my first team was in place. We now had to make the coalition Government work because that's what the people of Wales wanted. Ieuan Wyn Jones and I got on with each other in a First Minister and Deputy context, and we still get on personally. It is a difficult situation, a larger party working with a smaller one – people's attention will instinctively be drawn to the larger party and assume they're the ones doing all the work. It's harder for the smaller party to get the attention it might well deserve. The electoral story of junior coalition partners is not normally a happy one, and that isn't lost on the people in government. So, there were tensions, of course, quite often due to individual members of both parties stirring and agitating. But such issues were always dealt with internally and never discussed publicly.

The one occasion when Ieuan and I had a particularly difficult time was over the fate of a primary school in Cardiff. We had opposite views on the issue and it was a challenging period. Cardiff Council had put forward a plan in 2010 to move Ysgol Treganna Welsh-language primary school in Canton from its existing building because it was so overcrowded. The way they wanted to tackle this problem was to swap Treganna with Lansdowne Primary School nearby. The effect of such a move would be to put Treganna children in a much bigger building, with room to spare, and to squeeze a bigger number of Lansdowne children into a smaller building. There were protests on both sides of the argument, and what added a definite degree of additional emotion to the whole thing was the involvement of the Welsh language on one hand and the fact that a large proportion of Lansdowne children were Muslim. Neither factor was central to the issue in hand, nor a consideration for the council who had made the decision. But these aspects still upped the stakes quite a bit. The case landed on my desk, in the end, and I couldn't see any logic to the proposed school swap at all.

But I was then branded a traitor for opposing the moving of Ysgol Treganna. Plaid Cymru were quite vociferous in their condemnation of me. I would constantly and consistently say that Lansdowne had 100 more children than Treganna, so if the building was too small for Treganna, how could it be all right for Lansdowne? The Treganna parents couldn't understand why I, as a Welsh speaker, could say no to the new plans for their school. But language wasn't the issue, and this was a good example of where it is made into an issue without cause. The Muslim community felt aggrieved by the plans as well. They felt as if they were being sacrificed to benefit the Welsh school. They felt ostracized.

There were protests and demonstrations in Cardiff, and further afield as well, including one during the Wales-wide cultural event, the National Eisteddfod.

I was away at the dedication of my best man's son in Staffordshire that weekend. While I was there, Plaid Cymru held an executive meeting and one resolution that came from it was deeming me outrageous in my decision to say no to the move for Ysgol Treganna. That evening, while enjoying a bottle of wine with my friends, Ieuan Wyn Jones rang me. He kept on repeating, with reference to his Executive, 'Ma' nhw'n flîn iawn am hyn.' I couldn't understand why Ieuan was saying that his Executive was sorry. Why would they say that? I almost said 'apology accepted'. Then it dawned on me. Ieuan is from North Wales, where the Welsh at times can be perceived as another dialect, due to accent and vocabulary. It isn't, really, but this instance was a good example of a difference. For him, 'flîn' meant 'angry'; for me, it meant 'sorry'. The whole school issue was resolved in the end, with a new proposal that suited both schools.

That was a good example of the reality of not just coalition, but coalition in a small organization. The Senedd is not like Westminster, where you can avoid people you don't like, disagree with, or both. You know in Cardiff that you will always be bumping into each other. It's very hard, then, to hold any long-term and deep grudges or animosity. It makes for co-operation, and it influences the way we get on with each other.

If someone in the chamber has a go at me, I will still talk to them outside the chamber, as normal, knowing that they were only doing their job when they criticized me. The exception to that is if someone attacks your character. That's different. I don't like that aspect of politics.

The main new item on the agenda for my first Government was increased powers for the Assembly and organizing a referendum on that issue. The call was for the Assembly to be able to draft bills and pass acts in the same way as Westminster, Northern Ireland and Scotland could. Ieuan was pushing me to have the referendum in March 2011. I was very nervous about doing so, as it was only two months before an Assembly election, and I preferred an Autumn referendum. So I knew that sticking to my preferred Autumn referendum could harm the relationship between Plaid and Labour. Once again, the opposition I faced on this issue also came from many of my colleagues in London. It's an open question, but I'm not sure we would have had a referendum if Gordon Brown had been returned as Prime Minister in 2010. When Brown was replaced by David Cameron, the path to hold the referendum became a lot smoother. The then Secretary of State for Wales, Cheryl Gillan, was dead against the referendum and all that it would call for, but her boss, Cameron, drove it through.

This issue was the first time we had to deal with a Conservative Government. I had had only a few inter-actions with Gordon Brown, who took over from Tony Blair, because he was gone before I was First Minister, but I've got to know him more since he left office. I find him to be very good company, a very principled man, with a great sense of humour. But you might not know that. His public persona is very buttoned-up, which does him a disservice.

The one official meeting I remember having with Brown was in London. I walked into the room desig-nated for us and it was set up very strangely. There was a table in the room, with flowers on it. I was led to sit behind it, facing out. When Gordon came in, he sat next to me, so we weren't facing each other at all. This is a common set-up in meetings in China, but not in the UK, where a chat on the settee is the norm. It was all a bit stiff and starchy. As I sat there, I looked out of the window and saw his children's trampoline, which was exactly the same one that my children had. I mentioned this to him and his tone completely warmed. We started talking about our respective children and he shared how difficult it was to bring his up in Downing Street.

So the referendum was given the go-ahead and we now had a campaign to organize and run. This one would be nothing like the 1997 campaign. There was no Yes and No campaign. All four party leaders in the Assembly were in favour of the increased powers the referendum would seek support for. The small minority who opposed the new powers weren't a large enough group to organize themselves into a full-blown campaign. Much of their opposition was scare-mongering along the lines of the increased powers being the start of the slippery slope to independence and raising fears about increased taxation.

I took part in a *Question Time*-type event as part of the campaign. We were in Blackwood. Roger Lewis, the former chief executive of the Welsh Rugby Union, was there with me on the Yes side of the argument. On the opposing side was Nathan Gill, former UKIP and now Brexit Party member, and Rachel Banner, a campaigner against further powers. A man stood up to ask a question, wearing a bright yellow fisherman's coat, for some reason. He started bluntly, 'I want to ask Carwyn Jones: will these new powers mean I have to pay more taxes?' 'No,' was my straight answer. He was flustered by this and felt the need to get back at me. 'That's just typical of a politician, isn't it? Waffle, waffle, waffle!'

The biggest focus for us was deciding on the wording of the question the referendum was to ask. Initially it was three paragraphs long. There was no way that was going to work! In the end, I decided on one simple question: Do you believe that all the laws that only affect Wales should be made in Wales?

The campaign was going very well and the opinion polls were showing a clear majority in favour of the new powers for Wales. So much so, in fact, that on referendum day it was difficult to get people out to vote because everyone thought the result was a foregone conclusion. That had some influence on the turnout, no doubt, as did the abysmal coverage from the UK media on an issue as important as this was. When I went to my polling station, I met a young man who had come home from the navy in order to vote. 'I've come home to vote for Wales,' he said.

A significant majority of the Welsh population did the same. As the results came in, and we saw a few areas saying Yes when we though they would say No, we knew things had gone well. In the end, 517,572 voted in favour and 297,380 against. Only Monmouthshire said No as a county, and that was by only 320 votes. In the devolution referendum of 1997 that county had been almost 2:1 against. That was quite a swing. Other areas of Wales that had rejected devolution in '97 had now actually voted in favour of these new powers for the devolved parliament.

As a result of the vote, the Welsh Assembly had law-making powers in twenty devolved areas. It had come a long way since it first opened its doors in 1999. The weak administrative body that had been established then was, just fourteen years later, a law-making parliament. It was, for me, the sign of a nation growing in confidence and, dare I say it, a sign of a people taking back control of their laws. It was with great pride that I could address jubilant supporters in the Senedd and say, 'Today an old nation came of age.'

TWELVE

The Green, Green Grass of Wales

ONE OF THE legacies I inherited from Rhodri Morgan
was the arrival of one of the world's biggest sporting
events in Wales. The Ryder Cup has been a keenly con-
tested world-class tournament between the best golfers
of the USA and Europe since 1979, and between the
USA and Great Britain and Ireland before that, way
back to 1927. It had been held in the UK on seventeen
occasions before 2010, but that year it was to come to
Wales for the very first time. It was a prestigious event
that put Wales on a very high-profile stage.

It was to be held at the Celtic Manor Resort in Newport, South-East Wales. The original mansion house
the resort had developed around has its origins back in
the heyday of the coal industry in South Wales, being
the home of a colliery owner and industrialist. It later
became a maternity hospital, where over 60,000 babies
were born. One of these babies was a boy called Terry

Matthews, who was born in 1943. He would become Wales' first billionaire, making his money in high-tech communications. The maternity hospital closed in 1977 and, three years later, Terry Matthews bought the building, turning it into a seventeen-bedroom luxury boutique hotel. For five years in a row it was nominated best hotel in Wales in the Egon Ronay Guide. But Terry had far bigger plans for the site. Over a period of years he built a new 400-bedroom hotel, a £10 million golf clubhouse and a new golf course. When all this was finished, he was extremely enthusiastic about hosting the Ryder Cup there. And he put his money where his mouth was. He invested a further £16 million to prepare the Celtic Manor Resort for a Ryder Cup invitation. This included developing a brand-new golf course, the Twenty Ten. This was the first time in Ryder Cup history that a course had been built specifically for the event. So, thanks to Terry Matthews, Wales left its mark on Ryder Cup history.

This was a great opportunity all round for Wales, as it would showcase us in a way not done before. The media presence in Newport itself would be considerable and the media attention worldwide would be huge. The build-up to it was intense, with a Welcome to Wales concert held in the then Millennium Stadium. The European and American teams were on stage as well, receiving a very warm Welsh welcome. We really wanted to pull out all the stops in terms of how we were marketing Wales to the world – the economic and promotional impact was immense if we got this right – but it was not without difficulty. We almost had to cancel that concert, for example, because it was proving difficult to get big stars with the budget we had available. And with the event just weeks away, we were nowhere close to a full bill and I was advised to call it off. It was one of those occasions when instinct and determination overruled sensible and well-meant advice – my view was that the reputational hit would have been too significant. I asked my officials to showcase local talent, and in the end we did just that, and we managed to pull in some of the bigger stars as well.

The tournament itself had a very Welsh start – the rain poured down! That didn't help in terms of the usual clichés about Welsh weather, and gave us another Ryder Cup first – losing a whole day's play to rain. By the time the Sunday morning came, there had been no play since the Friday. There was even talk of abandoning the tournament. I was given this news as I was having breakfast with the American Ambassador, Louis Susman. That was not what we wanted the Ryder Cup in Wales to be remembered for. The situation was exacerbated further by the news that some of the spectator stands had become potentially unsafe, as they stood in rain-soaked mud. But the looming disaster was averted through a huge effort by those who were working on the course. Their diligence was then rewarded by the weather gods, as the rain finally relented and the sun did indeed shine down on the righteous.

It would have been incredibly unfortunate if we'd had the event cancelled, as we already have to put up with sniffy cricket journalists getting used to Cardiff hosting international cricket. They glory in every drop of Welsh rain during Test matches, as though Old Trafford, Edgbaston and Lords never lost a day's play to rain. As it turned out, it was one of the most exciting, memorable and hard-fought Ryder Cups there's ever been.

Europe eventually won the Ryder Cup and the whole event ended on a high note. The one statement that I still treasure to this day is the one made by European team captain Colin Montgomerie at the end. The world was watching, he said, and Wales delivered!

It was my responsibility to bring the proceedings to a close with a speech, which had been scripted some time in advance. But, on the day, I started to think again. I knew that people would be leaving the event with certain impressions of me and of Wales, based on what I said and how I said it. With that in mind, I thought that reading a prepared speech would not be appropriate. It would

Me, my parents and my
great-grandmother, Jane Lloyd,
who died a few weeks after
this photo was taken.

My mother and me.

With my parents at
New Quay.

Great-grandparents James and Elizabeth Jones. Their son, Henry-Tom, is pictured (*below*) on his wedding day to my grandmother, Catherine.

My maternal grandparents, Leslie and Rona Howells.

Age 2, holding what looks like a microphone but is actually a broken helicopter!

Age 7, when I had my stage debut as narrator in the school play.

Age 9, with Swci the Westie.

Age 20 at Dyffryn Gardens, Cardiff.

1987 – A protest at the Secretary of State's office, outside what was then the Welsh Office (little did I know that I'd be sitting in it twenty-five years later). I'm circled in yellow, and my friend Dave Taylor, with the cigarette, is circled in the red. He had told his mother he'd packed in smoking!

⬤ Members of the National Union of Students protesting against education cuts.

Education cuts protest

My first election in 1999,
on the campaign trail
in Porthcawl.

The young candidate!

Lisa's parents, Stella and Eddie Murray.

With good friends on mine and Lisa's wedding day. We're watching Barbarians v South Africa on a black-and-white TV.

Lisa at Aberystwyth
'kicking the bar'.

With the family at
my grandmother's
90th birthday.

At Disneyland Paris in 2009.

Calum, myself and Owen launching the 2015 Election campaign
in Ammanford.

With my father on the day I became FM.

be too formal. So I put the script aside and decided to speak off the cuff, in the hope that this would be warmer and more friendly. Before I made the speech, I spoke to legendary Welsh rugby player Gareth Edwards. I promised him that I would somehow mention his home village of Gwaun Cae Gurwen in my speech. If that place name sounds familiar, it's because it's part of the story of my ancestry. Gareth didn't believe for a second that I would manage to find a justifiable reason to include the name of a small West Wales village in my Ryder Cup speech, but I was determined.

I gave my speech and thanked Sir Terry Matthews, the teams, and all those who had come to Wales to enjoy the tournament. I said that it had been a pleasure to welcome people from all over the world to every corner of Wales and we would be proud to invite them back again 'from Buckley to Bridgend, from Porthmadog to Porthcawl, from Bangor to Brynaman and from Gaerwen to Gwaun Cae Gurwen'. I had succeeded in ticking off my parents' home village, my own hometown, and kept my promise to Gareth Edwards!

But more importantly, of course, the 25,000 or so in the audience, and the millions watching on TV, had heard the First Minister of Wales bringing an international event to a close. This is the sort of event that Wales would never have been able to host before the days of devolution. We would not have had the wherewithal to do anything on this scale. The course and facilities could well have been available, but we wouldn't have had the government to drive it through. The event was a huge boost, not only for golf tourism in Wales, but tourism in general. When the dust had settled and we had an opportunity to calculate the overall benefit of the Ryder Cup to Wales, we saw that it had been worth £100 million to the Welsh economy.

In 2011, there was an Assembly election, which we went into with a fair bit of confidence – the referendum result had put a spring in our step. In Westminster, the Conservative Government there was going through a period of being very unpopular, which helped the Labour cause in Wales. We set out five main pledges in our manifesto, covering the key areas of public concern. As ever, the big challenge came in how to explain this, our values and our manifesto, in a single memorable slogan that would attract people's attention. This generated a lot of debate. We chose one that is still being used to this day: Standing Up For Wales. This was a significant moment in the development of Welsh Labour, as a made-in-Wales political entity in our own right. It felt right, from the very first moment, and the fact that the party is still using it today says a lot about how well it works for Welsh Labour, and for modern Wales.

The pain of those discussions didn't start and stop with the English-language version, however. There was no simple straight translation into Welsh that would make sense in the various dialects. The North and South have different words for 'up', for a start. In the end, after discussion with my father, we agreed on a Welsh idiom, *Sefyll Cornel Cymru* – Standing in Wales' Corner. Even this wasn't uncontroversial. When it was first unveiled at our party conference, a number of Welsh speakers in the BBC started grumbling about whether it was grammatically correct. In the end, Betsan Powys, the then political editor of BBC Wales, confirmed that this was indeed a well-known Welsh idiom that made sense in our context.

As it turned out, we were as good as our word in that election campaign. We got stuck into the Conservative record in Westminster and showed how we would protect Wales from various cuts – by designing our own employment programme, for example. We gained four seats, taking us to a total of thirty, matching our high-water mark of 2003, but this time thanks to a singularly Welsh campaign, not a 'Blair bounce'.

The Conservatives, under Nick Bourne, gained two seats, taking them up to fourteen, although the vagaries of the electoral system meant that he lost his own seat. I phoned him the following day and he was philosophical about it, but it was harsh that gaining more seats in the constituency vote meant losing in the regional vote, and as Nick was a regional AM, he lost out. Nick, as a supporter of devolution, had taken the Conservatives a long way to becoming a genuinely Welsh party during his time in charge and he was undoubtedly a loss to the Assembly. Plaid Cymru lost four seats and the Lib Dems lost one. They had a total of eleven and five seats respectively. So, once again we were the largest party by far, but short of a majority, this time by one. Personally, I held my seat and tripled my majority in 2011. So I was back as First Minister. That is never something you can take for granted.

WELSH LABOUR	Carwyn Jones	13,499	56.2	+15.9
CONSERVATIVE	Alex Williams	6,724	28.0	−1.9
PLAID CYMRU	Tim Thomas	2,706	8.6	−6.0
LIB DEMS	Briony Davies	1,736	7.2	−8.0
Majority		6,775	28.2	+17.8
Turnout		24,035	40.8	+0.4

Given the strength of our performance, it may have been a moot point anyway, but Plaid Cymru quickly made it clear that they weren't interested in forming another coalition. The electoral history of junior coalition parties is a difficult one, and I think Plaid certainly felt their campaign struggled to get out of the shadow of their time in government. Frankly, I feel they spent far too much time attacking a record for which they were partly responsible, and should have been proud of delivering. As a consequence, the Labour Group were firmly supportive of forming a government on our own, and because of the referendum result, this was now a government that could pass laws. It was certainly a turning point; it was a good result for us and, with the other parties all in some form of disarray, we were confident in our ability to govern.

Within a few months, though, I was dealing with an event that we thought we'd seen the last of in Wales. On 15 September 2011, I was still on a visit to the Dyfed-Powys Police headquarters when a message came through that there had been an accident underground and men were missing. It was so unreal to hear these words at this point in history that I assumed it was some kind of exercise. Sadly, it became clear very quickly that this was a real emergency – at the Gleision Colliery above Pontardawe in the Swansea Valley.

I got to the site as soon as I could. It was not the kind of mine you picture with your mind's eye. There was no winding gear or a spake and colliery buildings to be seen. It was little more than one small hole in the hillside through which men had walked, and worked within, to win coal.

In the nearby village hall in Rhos, I met the families of the men who were still missing. It was one of the hardest things I've had to do. You can't give people false comfort; you can't say everything will be okay. You can only listen. Those men didn't survive, I'm sorry to say, and their families had to grieve. The ghosts of our mining history had come back to haunt us for one last time.

2012 WAS THAT historic year in which the first two Welsh Acts were passed. They were particularly significant acts, with historical relevance. The first of the two was the Official Languages Act, which provided for equality between the Welsh and English languages and was a significant piece of legislation as far as Welsh identity and self-belief were concerned.

The second was the Local Government Byelaws Act, a rather bland title for something that turned out to be very significant. It led to the very first battle in court between the UK Government and the Welsh Government. The UK Government argued that Wales didn't have the powers to change the ways that local government byelaws were made, without their consent.

We argued that we did, and the judges agreed with us. The issue was that the byelaws in question were applicable in Wales, only and only touched incidentally on the powers of Whitehall, so therefore came within the powers of the Welsh Government. Of course, that's a gross simplification of a long judgment, but, believe me, it was important.

My responsibilities as First Minister also meant representing Wales outside of the country as well as within. I had two major occasions to do so after the 2011 election. The first was a great pleasure for me: representing my country at the Rugby World Cup. Okay, I wasn't playing, but I was there. I went to New Zealand for the start of that year's tournament.

I was also invited back for the final if Wales got that far. We nearly, *nearly*, did! We narrowly lost to France in the semi-final, 9–8, in a game remembered for a controversial refereeing decision that saw Welsh captain Sam Warburton sent off after only nineteen minutes of the game. The referee was Alain Rolland, who, despite his name, was Irish. Believe it or not, I'm actually a qualified rugby ref, but as the game got quicker the, er . . . less mobile refs like me dropped out. At the risk of upsetting a number of rugby fans, I think Alain was right. In any other game Sam would have been sent off and it wouldn't have been right to make an exception. There,

I've said it. It was harsh for Sam, who had been a great captain and was far from being a dirty player.

I think Wales would have won the World Cup that year if we'd nailed our kicks and hadn't lost that semi. The invitation to the final had been sent by John Key, the New Zealand PM, whom I'd met earlier in Wellington. I would have been accompanied by Rob Holmes, a great guy who worked in my office. He was there at the semi-final and turned to me with despair on his face after the final whistle. He looked like someone who'd seen Willie Wonka's golden ticket fall apart in his hands!

During my earlier visit to New Zealand, I'd visited the Welsh Dragon Bar in Wellington, the only Welsh bar in the country. The fact that it occupied a former public toilet didn't diminish its charm, or the welcome. The owners had come from Swansea to visit New Zealand and they loved the place so much they'd decided to stay. During our chat they told me that their dog had died and they couldn't bring themselves to bury him in foreign soil, so they'd taken the body back to Wales to be buried. I asked them what sort of paperwork there was to take the body of an animal on the plane. They told me that they packed the dog in a case and then simply informed the authorities at the airport. They could see the disbelief on my face, but they were absolutely insistent, telling me it was before 9/11 and the strict security that followed. To this day I've never worked out if it was a wind-up or not.

The next occasion to represent Wales was slightly closer to home, at the London Olympics of 2012. The hosting of the Olympics was a legacy of Tony Blair's time in government, which might well have been forgotten by now. It was an occasion that would absolutely be of benefit to Wales as well, there was no doubt in my mind about that. I was invited to the opening ceremony along with Lisa. We went on one of the official buses to the stadium, and were in good company: Ed Miliband was with us, the then leader of the Labour party and also the leader of the opposition at the time, as well as Boris Johnson, then Mayor of London, Tessa Jowell MP, the Archbishop of Canterbury, top brass from the army and navy, and representatives of the Northern Irish Executive and Scottish Government.

But the driver got lost. We were going to be late arriving at the largest sporting event in UK history, in Boris's city. I watched Boris Johnson get more and more agitated as time went on. It was very soon a case of adieu to his bonhomie. He was seriously losing his patience, ranting at someone on his mobile and constantly telling everyone not to tweet anything about the situation we were in. We continued to circle the bright red 'observation tower', a structure made by famous artist Anish

Kapoor and structural designer Cecil Balmond, as it came into view only to quickly recede again. So near but yet so far. After several frantic calls by the driver for directions, we finally arrived there in time – just – and shared the same box as the royal family. It was an incredibly special feeling to represent Wales as a nation in its own right at the world's biggest sporting event. Remembering the sense of goodwill and international solidarity that coursed through the veins of people up and down the land at that time, it seems a different country from the one that voted to leave the European Union just four years later.

The Wales abroad theme continued at this time with the Welsh Government's dealings over Cardiff International Airport. We were aware that Wales' only International Airport, and our link with the world, in that sense, was not performing very well. It was losing flights. The airport buildings themselves desperately needed maintenance, and it was understaffed. Too many Welsh people chose not to fly from there. The airport at that time was owned by the Spanish company Abertis. They were world leaders in toll road management, and the airport industry was subsequently not one of their leading interests. We held numerous meeting with them, many chaired by me. The figures were quite straightforward. By the time we stepped into those negotiations, passenger numbers had dropped five years in a row. But Abertis didn't seem to be that concerned, as it wasn't their main focus as a company. They had bought Cardiff Airport as part of a package that included other airports. I think it's fair to say that they were quite happy with the way things were going at Cardiff, as long as they weren't losing a lot of money. They seemed to have no interest in investing, or in working with us. They just stated that regional airports everywhere were in decline and that's just how things were. At one point, they literally shrugged their shoulders at me, implying that Cardiff would go the same way.

We suggested they put the airport up for sale, but they would lose face if it went to another private company. Another dead end. But discussions continued and they finally came to a point where Abertis offered to sell the airport to us. This happened in 2013, and that had certainly not been our intention when the discussions had started, but it was clear that they thought such an approach was the best option for them, as it would allow them to save face with their competitors. Sale to a government implied an element of nationalization, which they were happy with. The price they asked, however, was ridiculous. We agreed to have an independent evaluation, which came up with a value of just over £50 million – way below the initial estimate.

So the Welsh Government bought Cardiff Airport. It was a risk, certainly, but a risk well worth taking. I have no doubt that it would have closed if we hadn't done so, leaving Wales as the only home nation without an international airport. It would have made the country smaller. The purchase also helped secure the British Aerospace Maintenance base, on the same site, and a total of a thousand jobs. At this moment, passenger figures have grown for the last four consecutive years, according to the Civil Aviation Authority, bringing Cardiff back to pre-2009 passenger levels. It also now offers flights to new destinations, the most significant of which is Doha, in Qatar. This wasn't even conceivable a few years previously. Much of that is due to the fantastic work of the then airport Chairman, Roger Lewis, and the Chief Executive, Debra Barber.

One thing I found on my travels outside Wales, or if I had conversations with leaders from other countries in Wales, was that being able to say we had an international airport was of crucial importance. If I had had to say that we didn't have such a facility, I might as well have said that we were in a backwater somewhere. It is of vital importance in order to attract business as well as to serve the population of Wales itself.

These first few years of the Welsh Government after 2011, in retrospect, could be seen as relatively straightforward. There wasn't the cut and thrust of elections, cabinet reshuffles, or even a referendum. I was selling Wales, hard, in a way that hadn't really been done before, and we were passing our own laws. Times were tough financially, but it was the normal business of government. In hindsight, though, while they weren't turbulent times, they were very significant years indeed as far as the story of Wales is concerned. We had passed our own laws. We had been officially represented at international events in our own right. The coming of age was moving on.

THIRTEEN

Body, Heart and Soul

THE OFFICIAL Welsh Government presence abroad was comprised of a set of offices scattered around the world. Wales had offices in New York, Washington, three in China, three in India, one in Tokyo, one in Dubai and one in Brussels. This sounds more impressive than the reality in some cases. There were offices, yes, but for some time there was no official structure co-ordinating our work abroad. For example, there was a Welsh office in New York and one in Washington, which consisted of only one person, but there was no link from one to the other and there was no central North America headquarters for the Welsh Government. Reports sent from our offices abroad were seen by civil servants but not by any Welsh Government minister.

It was obvious that things had to change. Having the correct representation abroad is crucial to being able to develop links with other governments and establish business connections. The Scots, already ahead of us in using the influence of their diaspora, had over ten times the number of representatives abroad as we had. We needed to address that imbalance.

The first thing I changed was making sure that all the monthly reports from all offices came directly to me. By doing that we stood a chance of singing from the same page. We arranged that the staff of these offices would meet up once a year to create a greater sense of belonging and camaraderie. In practical terms, the restructuring meant that in North America, for example, Washington was chosen as the headquarters, with the North American director based there. New York would deal with the cultural and financial side of our activities. An office was opened in Chicago, one in Atlanta to deal with the South, one in San Francisco to deal with tech issues, and one in Montreal to give us a Canadian presence. All these offices are co-ordinated from Washington.

This has made a huge difference. Before this, we had no political presence in the heart of American government at all. Now we have a caucus of over twenty congressmen who take an active interest in matters relating to Wales. Once a year, Wales hosts an event on Capitol Hill which showcases our nation right at the centre of American government. The level of trade we do with the US should make this kind of engagement an absolute no-brainer, but still there are doubters about the importance of this kind of outreach work.

We also needed to change the way we did things in Europe, as we were over-reliant on our offices in Brussels. It was too big an area to cover from one office, so we extended our reach through new offices in Paris, Berlin and Düsseldorf. We increased our staff in the Dubai office too, and opened an office in Doha as well. We also opened an office in Dublin and, perhaps not coincidentally, it was great to see that Ireland has now reopened its full-time consulate in Cardiff. All those years of me badgering them about it seems to have paid dividends. Closer to home, we also opened offices in London – fixing another glaring gap in our ability to reach out and exert influence beyond our own border. The London office has made a big difference in terms of being able to sell Wales, to attract business to Wales and in establishing a distinctly Welsh identity.

Despite the differences of political leadership, our offices across the world don't work in competition with the UK Government – far from it. We have been able to develop a good and mutually beneficial working relationship. In many cases, the Welsh office is in the UK embassy. I never experienced any awkwardness or opposition from any of the UK embassy staff, and when asked my opinion about domestic matters by people abroad, I gave my view, and not that of the Westminster Government. It was always made clear that Wales was a nation within the UK and that we were working together.

Back home, with the government agenda being delivered without too many bumps in the road, I decided that a reshuffle was needed in March 2013. I always felt that it was important to bring in fresh ideas and talent on a fairly regular basis, because governments can get stale and too reactive. One of the new additions was Mark Drakeford, as Minister for Health and Social Services. Normally I wouldn't bring anyone straight into the Cabinet unless they'd already had government experience as a deputy minister. Mark hadn't had that, but he had a great deal of experience as special adviser for Rhodri Morgan, and it's because of this that I wanted to bring him in earlier than usual.

The other changes involved brining in Alun Davies as Minister for Natural Resources and Food, as well as giving Edwina Hart an extension to her role, so she became Minister for Economy, Science and Transport. John Griffiths moved from environment to culture and sport. This was a mini reshuffle, just to give the Cabinet a bit of new impetus, but with no drastic changes. That was to happen a few months later, and unexpectedly.

It was around this time that I ran into my first really

difficult situation with a member of my Cabinet. There was a particularly awkward proposal being considered to reorganize the A&E provision in some Welsh hospitals. It involved Prince Charles Hospital in Merthyr, Princess of Wales Hospital in Bridgend, and the Royal Glamorgan near Llantrisant. There were three ministers in the Cabinet who represented the areas where these hospitals were, including me. This situation needed to be addressed, and at a Cabinet meeting I said that not one of us was to get involved with any local campaign relating to the proposed hospital changes in our areas. We were to remain silent on the issues until the review we had commissioned delivered their findings on the changes. This is always a difficult thing to balance, and I think the media and people outside of politics have a tough time understanding just how much pressure elected representatives can feel when it comes to contentious local issues. Unless it's your patch, you tend to look at the bigger picture and wonder why people with a national role get so involved in local issues. Difficult though it was, however, we agreed a way forward.

But within just a few days, Leighton Andrews was photographed protesting, carrying placards during a protest at his local hospital, the Royal Glamorgan. He was supporting the hospital's position. As I saw it, this went against what we had discussed in Cabinet. The option was there for me to ask him to step down, there and then. Maybe I should have done so, but instead I gave him a warning and he stayed in the Cabinet. A yellow card.

A few days later, it was brought to my attention that Leighton had also been campaigning against the closure of a local school in his constituency. This was after he had been very vocal in demanding that local authorities close small and unviable schools. This, on top of the previous incident, gave me a great deal to consider. Two yellows mean a red. I couldn't come to any other conclusion – Leighton's position was now untenable. So, on 25 June, I had to ask him to resign from the Cabinet. He took it very well, I have to say, and he didn't cause any problems as a result of my action. We stayed in touch, and I always made it clear that, with the passage of time, I'd want to see him back in government. And he was a real loss, because he'd been pushing through education reform that was long overdue.

I now had another reshuffle on my hands. I moved Huw Lewis from housing to be Minister for Education and Skills. Huw's characteristic response to me inviting him to take on that position was, 'Oh bugger!' I understood why he said that. Huw sometimes didn't have enough belief in his own capabilities, which are considerable, and he was also inheriting a whole load of scraps that Leighton had started with the sector. Jeff Cuthbert came in as Minister for Communities and Tackling Poverty. On the deputy ministerial side I brought Vaughan Gething in as Jeff's deputy. Ken Skates was Deputy Minister for Skills and Technology, meanwhile. These two were both bright young politicians who gave the Cabinet fresh new input and added some more energy. Reshuffles that you are forced into can be difficult, but, as it happens, I think this one worked out well and gave the team a good balance.

Talented though they were, the Cabinet was facing a tough period. With the age of austerity still in fashion at Westminster, it meant less and less money for the Welsh budget. Consequently, cuts had to be made to various departments, which put us under pressure not of our making. Health was a good case in point. We were given less money by the Conservative Government in London but were then criticized for making cuts in Wales by the Conservatives in the Assembly. In reality, we spent more per head on health than their party were doing in government in England. But this was the issue identified early on by the Tories as a weak spot to target during the campaigning for the 2015 General Election, and they worked away on that for a few years before the election came. They even succeeded in getting some of the London papers on board and it was difficult for us to rebut what they were saying about us.

The major legislative success of that time was passing the Human Transplantation Act. This followed a
very long and considered debate on whether we should
change the consent terms for organ donation. There had
been Government-organized public debates throughout
Wales on the issue as far back as 2008 and 2009. The
status quo was that people opted in to the system, saying
that they were happy to have their organs used after
their death. We wanted to consider giving people the
option to opt *out* of the scheme, working on the basis
of presumed consent unless notified otherwise. The Bill
went through several stages, and in the end over seventy
amendments were made. But it was passed, under the
guidance of Mark Drakeford, and hospitals in Wales can
now presume that people in Wales who are over eighteen
want to donate their organs after they die. This is the
most significant legislation that the Welsh Government
has passed. Wales was the first country in the UK to
introduce this scheme. There aren't many pieces of legislation that save lives, but this one does.

AT HOME, Seren was entering her teenage years. Up
until then, all was relatively harmonious, for her as well
as for us, but this time in her life proved very difficult.
Like any other teenager, she was facing issues relating to her own identity. But Seren also faced the not

unexpected dilemma of wanting to know who her birth parents were, as well as the darker shadows that coming to terms with being adopted can understandably bring. It's fair to say that it was a real battle for her, which affected every aspect of her life. She found it difficult to go to school – and to be there, when she did. Lisa and I were extremely concerned about this emotional turmoil she was going through. While Ruairí has not shown any interest at all in knowing who his birth family is, Seren got to the point of resenting being adopted. It's a natural reaction for a young person, but it was difficult for us all to deal with at the time.

This was a significant period of adjustment for us all. Seren primarily had to come to terms with some deep-seated issues within herself. We had to watch her go through this and learn how to adjust and adapt ourselves. There were times when we were completely at a loss. We discussed if I should continue my role as First Minister, in the light of what was going on at home. Maybe I needed to be at home more? As far as the effect on me, personally, it was a trying time in that I had to learn how to deal with real stress in work and real stress at home at the same time. I'm not saying this was unique to me, of course. In the end, we decided against my stepping down and that we should concentrate instead on keeping the status quo as much as we could.

But Seren pulled through it. She's a different person now: a confident, ambitious young woman, in a way that I didn't think at one point would be possible. That period of difficulty she went through did affect her schooling, however – especially at GCSE – but she made the decision to go to Cardiff and Vale College. Taking this step, which involved travelling to Cardiff every day, has been the making of her. She completed a number of courses while she was there. During one of those courses, Lisa and I acted as guinea pigs for her assessments. Lisa had a lovely time, with head massages and relaxation. I, on the other hand, was subjected to various forms of electrocution for three hours for some obscure purpose, and any complaint was met with a demand to 'man up'! She has moved on from that to the world of work and has definite plans for the next years of her life.

My health was not particularly good at this time, either. Just before a holiday in 2012, I began to notice that my joints were really stiff when I woke up in the mornings. On the holiday, I found that it was easier if I slept at night with my arm tied to the bedpost above my head, as this would ease the pain in my shoulder. When I got up I would have to shuffle around for the first hour or so until the joints loosened. The GP sent me to see a specialist, who confirmed that I had rheumatoid arthritis, and I was told that there were drugs that could slow the process down and ease the pain. I started with Methotrexate, which meant that I had to start injecting myself once a week. That wasn't as bad as I feared. But I got to the point where, whenever I smelt the antiseptic wipes, I would gag immediately. They then changed the medication, thankfully. For years after that I had no pain at all in my joints.

When I finished as First Minister in 2019, I went back to the specialist to ask what the situation was with my rheumatoid arthritis. He examined me. He did some blood tests. He then said that everything was clear. It had gone completely. I assumed he meant that the drugs had managed to suppress it sufficiently for me to feel no pain. 'No,' he said, 'the rheumatoid arthritis itself has gone, there is no trace of it. The bloods are completely clear.' I couldn't believe it. It had vanished.

Where the rheumatoid arthritis came from, we don't know. It could have been stress-related and, when that stress had gone. the arthritis went with it. It's possible. I'm a lucky person, if so.

FOURTEEN

Security and Independence

FOUR YEARS AFTER Wales welcomed the Ryder Cup, we were to play host to another massive international event. NATO chose Wales as the venue for its Summit in 2014. It was the first NATO Summit since Chicago in 2012 and the first in the UK since Margaret Thatcher hosted one in 1990. This meant delegates coming to Wales from dozens of countries around the world. The 2014 meeting happened against the backdrop of NATO's longest ever mission, the one in Afghanistan, and the growing tensions between Russia and the Ukraine. These two conflicts gave a definite significance to this particular gathering. NATO needed to assert its authority at a time when significant world events were threatening it. Just as European Ryder Cup captain Colin Montgomerie said that the world was watching in 2010, so it was our turn again to put our best foot forward in 2014. NATO was watching, as well as the world. Many of the world's leaders came to Wales and it was fascinating to meet them. François Hollande was aloof, Tayyip Erdoğan softly spoken, and Angela Merkel was very engaging. Then, of course, there was Barack Obama. He had a certain casual style about him that hid a formidable intelligence. A great ambassador for his country. How times have changed.

But before any of that could happen, and while the arrangements for it were still taking place, there was a lot of activity in both the Welsh and Scottish Parliaments. We passed quite a few Acts that year, one of which was the Agricultural Wages Act. Again, this was another seemingly straightforward piece of legislation, but it saw us in court again, once more taking on the Westminster Government. The issue was whether the Agricultural Wages Board was devolved or not. We argued that it was part of agriculture, therefore it was devolved. Westminster argued that it was part of employment, so it wasn't devolved. The judges once again agreed with us. That was an important victory, and set a helpful precedent for the future.

One of the main driving forces behind this Act was Alun Davies, the Minister for Natural Resources. We both went back a long way, back to our student days in Aberystwyth, when Alun was a fiery member of Plaid Cymru. Alun's fiery temperament had cooled a little since those days, but he could still find ways to land himself in trouble, and that led to a difficult series of events in government, later in 2014. Firstly, Alun had been in correspondence with the Environment Agency on a local issue. But he hadn't made it sufficiently clear that he was doing so as an AM, and not as a minister. That is a crucial difference, as approaching the agency as a minister could be interpreted as putting undue pressure on a government body that was funded from his own department.

Other parties found out and drew my attention to this breach of the ministerial code. I took the view that a reprimand would be enough – another yellow-card offence. Unfortunately, it was then brought to my attention that Alun had tried to obtain details of some of the farming subsidies that opposition party politicians were receiving. He didn't obtain that information, but the very fact that he had tried to obtain it meant that it was serious. That wasn't something that I could ignore, because if it came to light later that I had known about it and hadn't said anything, then my head would be on the block. I had to remove him from the Cabinet. Rebecca Evans was brought into the Cabinet in his place, as Deputy Minister for Agriculture and Fisheries. At the time, Alun did not take it well at all. He couldn't see any justification for my action. It's true to say that it harmed the relationship between us for several years, but thankfully that friendship has since been repaired. In fact, I think his experience of having been on the end of a difficult decision with which he disagreed gave him a huge amount of perspective at the time of the Carl Sargeant tragedy. He offered me valuable support at that time, even though I know he was under external pressure to go after me.

Earlier that year, a bill was introduced to the House of Commons that led to the Wales Act 2014. This was a response to the findings of the Silk Commission, led by Sir Paul Silk. Again, the brief was to see if there were ways to extend devolution in Wales. That happened and, as a result, stamp duty, business rates and landfill tax were devolved as well. We were also given some responsibility over income tax, and now a third of income tax raised in Wales stays in Wales. We also gained increased powers over Assembly elections.

But we were disappointed that we weren't given more powers over the justice system, which stayed with Westminster. That wasn't the case for the Scottish and Northern Irish justice systems, which were devolved. Wales is the only one of the four UK nations that doesn't run its own justice system. For the lawyers out there, England and Wales is the only jurisdiction where there are two Parliaments. Without going into too much detail, it means that somebody could be arrested, and possibly tried, in England for an offence committed in Wales even if it isn't an offence in England. In May this year, the Welsh Parliament will be the only one anywhere without the ability to enforce its own laws. It's a nonsense that will have to be addressed pretty soon.

This was also the Act that finally gave us the official name that we had always wanted. Any permutation of Welsh Assembly or Welsh Assembly Government was now gone and we were finally, officially, the Welsh Government. I had already changed it unofficially in 2011, because I just didn't like the name Welsh Assembly Government. It wasn't called the English Parliament Government, so why should we have a different kind of name?

2014 was also the year of the Scottish Independence referendum. The Scottish people were asked a big question: 'Should Scotland be an independent country?' The answer options were a simple Yes or No. The turnout on voting day showed that this issue had really exercised the Scots: 86% of them voted, the highest turnout in a referendum or an election since universal suffrage was introduced. Apart from any other historical and constitutional implication, this had a direct bearing on the NATO conference that Wales was preparing for. If the referendum was successful, and Scotland voted for independence, then it would be the dominant issue at the NATO Summit.

The Scottish referendum was an historical event in its own right, though, whether there was to be a NATO conference in the UK the same year or not. Scotland had been a part of the Union since 1707. The fact that one of the four nations of the UK was considering breaking away was in itself significant. If Scotland went on its own, what would happen to the UK? What would that mean to the other three nations that made up the British state? It was a time when we had to seriously consider constitutional questions that we hadn't before.

I spent a great deal of time in Scotland during that year. I was there campaigning for a No vote, because I thought that four individual nations within one state was the best way forward. I didn't feel that Scotland had to be independent to be more Scottish. I met SNP leader Alex Salmond many times during this campaign. He was a larger-than-life character, who liked to talk a great deal. He was very avuncular, but I don't think he ever forgave me for going up to Scotland to campaign against him. Up to that moment we had been on the same side on a number of battles with the UK Government, but there was no way I wasn't going to support my colleagues in Scottish Labour. The SNP were dominant at that time. They had recently hosted the Commonwealth Games and were happy with the bounce that would give them. In terms of timing, and political management in the run-up to the referendum, they couldn't have worked it much better.

It nearly succeeded, but not quite. The result showed 2,001,926 against and 1,617,989 in favour. I think the SNP got two issues fundamentally wrong. One was pensions. They hadn't quite worked out what would happen to people in Scotland who had pensions in UK funds. The other was currency. There seemed to be an insistence by the SNP that they would keep sterling and they would have a seat on the board of the Bank of England. I could never understand that. How could one country have a seat on the board of a bank in another? I think this is one of the key reasons they failed to get over the line. And, certainly, Alistair Darling, former Chancellor of the Exchequer and, at that time, Edinburgh West MP, pushed home the point in his head-to-head encounters with Salmond at the time.

And so, with the UK still intact, NATO came to Wales. For the first time ever, a sitting American president came to Wales as well. That in itself was an indication of the logistical issues we had to deal with to make the conference function properly. Wherever Barack Obama went, he had a convoy of about thirty vehicles with him, including his own medical vehicle.

It was the Foreign Office of the UK Government who were responsible for organizing the conference, but they made sure to involve us every step of the way.

When Barack Obama arrived at the Celtic Manor in Newport, again the host venue for a major event, he travelled in the same car as David Cameron. As things turned out, Obama stepped out of the car on the side where I was standing, with Stephen Crabb, Secretary of State for Wales, on the other side, where Cameron came out. I went towards Obama, shook his hand, welcomed him and introduced myself. When Cameron came around to our side of the car, he stretched out his arm and introduced me to Obama, saying, 'This is Carwyn Jones, First Minister of Wales,' unaware that I had already introduced myself. The President and I were busy talking and, consequently, I didn't notice Cameron or his outstretched arm. To the watching world, it looked as if Cameron had reached out his hand for me to shake and I had refused to do so. It looked as if I had snubbed him completely. I had many, many messages about that – some pulling my leg, and some congratulating my seemingly rude behaviour. The next time I saw the Prime Minister, I assured him it wasn't a calculated snub.

The summit was a great event to showcase Wales and to show that we were thriving as a nation. We could show off the Celtic Manor and Cardiff Castle as two exquisite but completely different locations. Wales hosted delegates from twenty-nine countries, as well as observers from others. We could never have done so before devolution. The financial benefit for Wales wasn't as great as it was from the Ryder Cup, but there were other substantial benefits from having world political leaders in Wales.

THAT AUTUMN there was another Cabinet reshuffle. They do seem to come along fairly regularly! My thinking is that a reshuffle, or a mini reshuffle at least, is needed about every eighteen months or so in order to keep our outlook fresh on the issues we deal with daily. In this particular reshuffle, I wanted to have a team in place well in advance of the Assembly election that would be held in 2016.

Jane Hutt stayed as Minister for Finance but took over as Leader of the House as well. Edwina Hart stayed where she was. This was also an opportunity to bring Leighton Andrews back into the fold after his dismissal. Although Leighton could be a difficult character, he was undoubtedly talented and I had told him he would be given another chance in government. There was a reforming job of work to be done, working with local government, and I hoped he could get it done, and so

I appointed him Minister for Public Services. Lesley Griffiths became Minister for Communities and Tackling Poverty, taking over from Jeff Cuthbert, who left the government. Carl Sargeant became Minister for Natural Resources and John Griffiths left the government at that stage. This was particularly difficult for me, as I'd known John for many years. But putting the best team together sometimes means losing those who you count amongst your friends. Vaughan Gething was moved to Deputy Minister for Health under Mark Drakeford. Ken Skates became Deputy Minister for Culture, Sport and Tourism under Edwina Hart. Rebecca Evans' brief was changed to Deputy Minister for Farming and Food, while Julie James came in as Deputy Minister for Food and Technology.

Gwenda Thomas, a long-serving AM, who by then was Deputy Minister for Children and Social Services, also left the government. Gwenda's huge strength was social services. She was a leader in her field in that respect. In 2014 she brought in the Social Services and Well-being Act, which was introduced to give a legal framework to improve life for people who need care and support. It came into force in 2016 and was a significant piece of legislation. I took the view that Gwenda had achieved her main goal, and exceeded it too. It was time, I thought, to give someone else a chance. It was a managerial decision and in no way a reflection on Gwenda herself. But I didn't deal with it very well and I hadn't reckoned with how upset she would be when I told her. She didn't want to leave government at all and I hadn't allowed for that. Gwenda is a wonderful person, and had done a great job – she was the last person I wanted to upset.

This was a particularly difficult reshuffle, as it meant, probably for the first time, that ministers were leaving the Cabinet who didn't want to do so. Previously, ministers had expected to be moved or taken out of government and in many cases had told me beforehand that they were prepared for it. This was different. But, it was also an important moment. Cronyism is one of the worst things that can happen to a government, and as a leader you have to watch yourself that you don't head that way almost by default. I know that Rhodri found it almost impossibly difficult to change up his ministerial teams – and it is very difficult in our small political world to ask someone, a friend, to step aside. But the alternative is worse. You always have to have the best team, and a team you trust.

SOME MONTHS later we were involved in a Westminster General Election. As polling day drew nearer, it was thought that Ed Milliband had a good chance and we could actually be working with a Labour Government again in Westminster. The polls certainly indicated as much and the public mood seemed to be reflecting the desire for change. However, in the last few days of the campaign things changed dramatically. Voters swung back to David Cameron. The Lib Dems were hammered and certainly suffered for being the junior partner in the previous government's coalition, and most of all for abandoning their pledge on tuition fees. The expectation of a Labour victory had brought with it the belief that austerity would come to an end. With Cameron's victory, however, came the definite confirmation that it was to continue. That had an immediate impact on the Welsh Government. It would affect our ability to provide local government with the resources they needed to run their services. Schools, highways, hospitals and so many other areas would feel the pinch. I must say that, publicly, the Labour Local Authorities in Wales did not blame the Welsh Government for this financial squeeze and thankfully saw it for what it was – the austerity agenda of the UK Government. We were always grateful for that response from our local government colleagues. We fought tooth and nail to provide them with the best settlements we could, with our budgets so stretched, but I know how tough it has been.

In increasing our financial responsibilities, the Wales

Act of 2014 had the added effect of giving us borrowing powers we'd not had before. We had, again, been different from all the other UK governments in that we weren't able to borrow any money. If there was a project that could only be financed by borrowing, then we couldn't do it, just because it was in Wales. This had put us at an obvious disadvantage.

2015 came to an end with the introduction of a ground-breaking piece of legislation, The Well-being of Future Generations Act. This was the fruition of many years' debate about embedding sustainability at the heart of government – something for which Jane Davidson has been a torch-bearer. The idea of sustainability legislation was a difficult concept to convey, however, and it passed through a number of official and political hands before taking shape. I think it was Huw Lewis who alighted on the idea of legislating to protect future generations – something he'd picked up from Germany. Even then it was a struggle to give clear definition to the Bill's aims. We just knew that the principle behind it was secure enough and that it would take some work to define it from there. It was based on the simple premise that we as a government needed to think more long-term and to encourage other public bodies to do so as well. How does what we do now affect the life chances of those to come after us? That was the key question we would encourage as many organizations as possible to ask. As the minister tasked with taking forward the Bill, Carl Sargeant did a very good job of keeping opposition members involved and informed. The Act was passed and the role of Future Generations Commissioner for Wales was established. This role encouraged long-term thinking about poverty, health inequalities and climate change, among other topics. Nowadays, other countries come to us to ask us how we run this aspect of our work.

But in the broader political picture, the General Election of 2015 put us under the cosh considerably. Milliband's defeat made us realize that we would have a fight on our hands when the Welsh Assembly election came in 2016. And then, of course, there was Brexit.

FIFTEEN

Brexit Means What?

THE DIFFICULTIES we faced as a Government in the run-up to the 2016 Assembly election weren't only related to the 2015 General Election defeat. We had our own situation to face up to in Wales. The Labour party had been in government for coming up to seventeen years by then. That in itself brought with it challenges of its own. There was a certain familiarity creeping in. The longer you're there, the easier it is for people to sell the message that it's time for a change. It then becomes ever more difficult to ensure that you can gain the faith of the electorate. Maybe people want a new party leading government? We knew we had our work cut out for us taking on this mindset alone, never mind all the stresses and strains that come with every election. There was certainly no way of taking anything for granted. It would be a difficult campaign. But, it was a campaign we were prepared for.

We learned a great deal from the 2015 General Election – in particular how people had reacted badly to a boringly 'safe' campaign from the UK party. The set-piece events, the whole style and feel of the campaign, felt overly managed and it stopped people engaging. This was certainly not lost on my campaign team, and I was hastily signed up to what I dubbed the 'masochism strategy' – essentially a public speaking and Q&A tour around Wales to give people the chance to shout at me. It was an opportunity a few of them took, to be fair, but generally speaking it all took place in the right spirit.

The first of these events was in Gower, a seat we lost in 2015, and one we knew the Tories would target strongly in 2016. Well, my advisers got what they wanted. After a few short words from me, we had a barrage of questions, and then someone stood up and started shouting the odds at me. The only thing slightly out of the ordinary is that he was a county councillor in my own borough. I was a bit unsure if this was the right thing to be doing, especially as the cameras were in the room. But, when I went backstage, my staff were grinning from ear to ear – no point in going out to show you're listening if no one gets to see what that looks like, they said.

And it was the right thing to do. As I said earlier, even if it couldn't be further from the truth, people could accuse you of complacency after being so long in charge – by turning up in people's town and village halls, and engaging with them completely on their own terms, we hopefully showed people the level of respect they were due. My political engagements were interspersed with Carwyn Connect events, with a similar aim – to show Government was listening. And Ken Skates, who I had asked to write the manifesto, did his own tour of Wales, gathering ideas for what was to be a very popular set of policy proposals. This kind of engagement really set the tone for our campaign, and from Day 1 we really did fight back the opposition and media narrative about it being 'time for change'. We looked more hungry and engaged than the opposition parties, and it was paying off. Under the campaign slogan 'Together for Wales', our local parties felt they had a fighting chance in all our key seats.

The electorate was not the only challenge, however. Ten days before polling day, Lisa had a slipped disc. She was admitted to hospital in Cardiff and was discharged once the problem was sorted. But while she was there she developed a kidney infection which went undetected. To help with the pain, she was prescribed Oramorph. Because of the infection, the morphine wasn't being cleared by the kidneys as it should have been. Instead, it built up inside her. On the Saturday night before the election, my daughter had been at a friend's house and rang me to ask for a lift home. This was at two in the morning. I went to fetch Seren and, when we arrived back at the house, I found Lisa mainly unresponsive and breathing strangely: she would breathe deeply, then wouldn't breathe at all for a minute or so. It's called Cheyne-Stokes breathing, a distinctive pattern associated quite often with the way people breathe at the end of their lives.

I called an ambulance and the paramedics took her to the Princess of Wales Hospital in Bridgend. Once there, they confirmed that she'd had a morphine overdose because of the build-up in her kidneys. She was given drugs to deal with this, and these meant that she would be to and fro between being alert and in some sort of coma. She was like that for a few days. I have no doubt that if I hadn't had to wake up in order to go and get Seren, Lisa wouldn't be with us today.

Focusing on any election campaign with that on my mind would have been very difficult; focusing on one that we knew would be so challenging made it even more so. For the first time, I started thinking seriously about whether I wanted a few more years as leader and First Minister. The nature of the campaign designed in Transport House was focused strongly on my leadership and on presenting me as the only obvious First Minister in the field. You might think that's a very flattering campaign strategy, but actually it puts a lot of pressure on you to perform day in, day out. I was the message carrier for all our most important campaign days: I was doing a lot of media, and doing the debates, and suddenly, with things so difficult at home, it was a hard burden to carry.

Much of this campaign was dominated by a debate about the growing steel crisis, and I even asked for the Assembly to be recalled in the early weeks of the campaign so we could discuss it. Tata Steel were in trouble, and with numerous plants and thousands of jobs at risk in different parts of Wales, it was a difficult and turbulent time for many of our communities. I was proud of how we responded to that – both politically and as a government. The commitments we made were never matched by interventions from the UK Government, though, interventions that would have cost them comparatively little, and I don't think that will ever be forgotten in Port Talbot, Llanelli, Newport and Shotton. We did everything we could to give those communities a second chance.

As polling day got closer, we prepared ourselves for losing seats. Despite the strength of the campaign, we almost started to believe the external narrative that change was coming, and with the party in a bit of a mess at a UK level, the electoral environment was challenging. Personally, I had decided that if we fell as low as twenty-five seats then I would resign. But as the results came in and the night drew on, it became apparent that we had achieved an extraordinary result, in the circumstances. In fact, the only seat we lost was a real shocker, where we lost the Rhondda to Plaid Cymru. Leighton Andrews' majority of 6,739 was turned into a majority of 3,459 for Leanne Wood, leader of Plaid Cymru. Leanne had a huge amount of national exposure in the 2015 General Election campaign, and that, combined with a tenacious local battle saw her achieve a result that masked an otherwise poor Plaid performance. The loss of the Rhondda meant we went down to twenty-nine seats overall, while Plaid gained only one and went up to twelve seats. The Conservatives ended with eleven seats, which was a loss of three. The Lib Dems went down to one, losing three seats that night. The new, grim factor in the equation was the success of UKIP, who won seven seats in the election.

We were once again in the situation of needing to work out how we were going to govern. We had managed on thirty seats, but it wasn't always easy. I was open to at least considering another coalition, and with the Lib Dems having all but disappeared, Plaid Cymru were the only available option. Leanne Wood was not so keen. But the message I had from Plaid was that if I was to put myself up for First Minister again, they wouldn't oppose it. I saw my priority as securing our position in government, which in effect meant that I needed to take us up to thirty members again. The obvious way for me to do so was to talk to the one Liberal Democrat that had been returned by that election. That was Kirsty Williams, Assembly Member for Brecon and Radnor, who had been in the Assembly since the beginning. She had also been leader of her party in Wales. I appointed her Education Minister. Kirsty and I had known each other for years and got on well. I knew she would make an excellent minister and I was right. Although our discussions about Kirsty joining the Government were fairly straightforward, that wasn't the case for Kirsty's discussions with her own party – she had a number of political hoops to jump through to secure the party's backing.

In our devolved system, the First Minister has to be voted back in as First Minister in the Assembly chamber. I didn't expect that to be an actual contest as we had been told by Plaid that, although they were not keen on coalition, they wouldn't stand in my way. But we soon got wind that Leanne Wood was actually thinking of standing against me as First Minister. And Plaid – Adam Price in particular – had been reaching out to the Tories, and even UKIP, to get them on board for the vote. As it turned out, my speaking to Kirsty and asking her to be in the Cabinet proved crucial to my staying on as First

Minister. I'm not sure at all what Plaid's thinking was in opposing me, as they only had twelve AMs. But when the votes were in, it was a tie. That's the way of politics and I never held a grudge about it.

There has been some reinterpreting of history about this episode, mind you. The first thing to say was that we went ahead with the vote, even after we got wind of Plaid's manoeuvring, in quick order and for good reasons. We were only months away from the referendum on our membership of the European Union, and with seven UKIP AMs having been returned to the Assembly, it was clear to all that we were facing a real battle. It was a battle I wanted to get into immediately. Secondly, we knew that with Kirsty's support the vote would be tied at the very worst, and we'd come back and vote again. We reckoned that the political damage for Plaid on only twelve seats, and doing deals with the Tories and UKIP, would be worse than for us, on twenty-nine seats, doing the right thing and trying to form a government to get on with things.

This period was also an occasion for another misinterpreted photo opportunity, like the one with Cameron during the NATO Summit. I had hay fever the day the results were announced. My eyes were streaming at one point, and I put a handkerchief over my face to stop my eyes running. This was just after the result had been announced. Of course, that was the photograph on the front page of the *Western Mail* the day after, with more than a slight implication that I was crying my eyes out because I hadn't won the vote to be First Minister. I was mortified! There's no way on earth that I would cry as a result of a tied vote like that. There are many reasons to be upset in life, but this was not one of them. I've always been philosophical about political wins and losses. But not so about front pages when it looks like I'm crying.

Two weeks of negotiations with Plaid led to a number of commitments from us regarding how we'd work with them on budgets and legislation. We'd lost two weeks campaigning, and, worse still, the relations between Plaid and Welsh Labour were now really strained just at the time when we should have been working together to fight off the UKIP challenge. It was a strange and awkward time between the two parties, and lines of communication kept dropping in a way that had never happened before. I think their poor election had really hurt them, and they were determined to find a new relevance. I always admired Leanne as a politician, and as a person, and we speak on friendly terms now, but we just were on different planets at that time. Whatever the thinking, the next vote went my way and I was to remain as First Minister. I now, finally, needed to form my third government.

We changed the job title from Minister to Cabinet Secretary at this point. Ken Skates was promoted to Cabinet Secretary for the Economy and Infrastructure, Vaughan Gething was Cabinet Secretary for Health, Well-being and Sport, Carl Sargeant was Communities and Children, Mark Drakeford became the Cabinet Secretary for Finance and Local Government, Lesley Griffiths was Environment and Rural Affairs, while Jane Hutt became the new Leader of the House and the Chief Whip, as Janice Gregory had stood down at the previous election. The Deputy Ministers, or Ministers, as they were now called, were: Julie James, Minister for Skills and Science; Alun Davies came back into the Cabinet as Minister for Lifelong Learning and the Welsh Language; Rebecca Evans was Social Services and Public Health; and Mick Antoniw was Counsel General. So, I was confirmed as First Minister and we had a government. We did know, however, that, because of the arithmetic, governing wouldn't be plain sailing.

But that wasn't the biggest challenge ahead. With the election behind us, we knew that there was a referendum looming to decide whether we were to stay in the European Union or not. We didn't foresee then how much that one referendum result would dominate politics for over three years. I had done everything short of getting down and begging David Cameron not to hold such a referendum six weeks after our election in Wales. We had spent months campaigning hard, knocking lumps out of each other politically. A referendum would call for cross-party collaboration. In addition, because of the work and effort of the Assembly election, we were already on our knees. We needed time to refresh, revitalize and regroup. I think David Cameron thought that he could win the referendum himself, and he didn't need to consider the help of the Welsh. More than that, I don't think he ever thought that Brexit would be a reality.

We faced another difficulty too, which was that, for many people, this seemed like an internal Tory psychodrama, with Gove and Johnson on one side and Cameron and Osborne on the other. The Labour Party didn't seem to engage much in the discussion in those early days, and with what was perceived by the public as a lukewarm approach from Jeremy Corbyn, we really failed to get a foot in the door in terms of shaping the campaign.

The conversations I had in various communities around Wales were illuminating, but often depressing. Some mentioned immigration, even though there was very little if any in the areas where they lived. To those who questioned how exactly they had gained from EU membership, I invariably pointed at things in their area funded by European money. Often I would have the reply, 'It's the Welsh Government who got that for us.' While it was gratifying to know that they could see the difference between what they had from Cardiff and from London, the projects we were talking about were financed by European money, even if we had directed how it had been spent. There is a lot of debate about how well we did as a country and a government celebrating those investments, but the European flag is badged on them all, and I don't think anyone in government over the two decades of devolution shied away from their pro-European values.

I think there were two factors that motivated the Leave voters in Wales, especially the Labour supporters amongst them. Firstly, they wanted to kick David Cameron. They thought it was a free hit. I don't know how many times I heard, 'Don't worry, Mr Jones, we're still Labour, but we'll vote Leave.' Cameron was always the target of such comments. The second factor was, in effect, a protest against globalization. Maybe it wasn't articulated in such a way, but that was the underlying theme. What I would often hear were comments such as, 'My dad worked in the mines, it was a tough job, but he had a pension, security, we knew where we were. Now, I'm in two jobs, I haven't got a pension and I don't know how long I'll be where I am.' The referendum was perceived as an opportunity to say 'Up yours!' to those who had created the world they lived in. People had a strong perception that they couldn't achieve such an end in a General Election, as a protest vote then might let the wrong party into government. But here, they felt, was a chance to say 'you're failing us' without, as many saw it, a direct impact on who made the decisions about their lives and services.

In the end, 51.89% of people in the UK voted to leave and 48.11% voted to remain. Greater London, Northern Ireland and Scotland all voted to remain. Wales voted to leave by 854,572 votes to 772,347. From that day until this, people have asked me why Welsh voters took such a direction. I've suggested a few reasons already. Another factor is that, unlike in Northern Ireland and Scotland, the Welsh tend to read the English newspapers, which were far more Eurosceptic. The *Scottish Sun* is not Eurosceptic at all, while the *Sun* in England is. The London papers don't bother to produce Welsh editions, an arrogance on their part, but also a sign of our weakness, given that most Welsh people continue to buy papers that don't bother to talk to them. This was another factor in why it would have been so important for Wales to have space between our own election and the referendum. What Scotland could do through its stronger media and civic society, we needed to do through hard work on the ground.

The result was clear, even if it was unexpected. But one other thing that was absolutely clear was that there was no plan for what to do next. There was no provision in the question the referendum asked that described in detail what would happen next. That is one contribution that the Welsh Government could have made, had we been asked and had our voice been listened to. We had held referenda in Wales before. When that happened, there was a document prepared to outline the consequences if there was a Yes vote. If the vote was for Welsh devolution, then the document explained what that meant and how it would work. No such document existed for the Brexit vote, an historic dereliction of duty for British democracy, and the consequences will reverberate for at least a generation. The interpretation as to what 'Leave' meant was wide open.

There was very little mention of Northern Ireland in the run-up to the referendum. I was keenly aware of the Brexit implications for that country, being married to an Irish woman. There was a distinct reluctance to listen whenever the question of the Irish border was raised. No one wanted to know. It often seemed strange coming from me, as First Minister of Wales; why was I the one banging the drum on the Irish issue when most of the country remained silent? But my personal connections, and the interest they engendered in Irish politics and history, made it seem like the most obvious, and intractable, problem with the whole idea of Brexit. The other side simply dismissed it, which suggested an old-fashioned imperialist arrogance among the Brexiteers that Ireland would fall in line and do what we wanted them to.

Cameron, in the aftermath, went and left Theresa May to sort everything out. I was now dealing with yet another Prime Minister. They were very different characters. And, in many ways, Theresa May was dealt an impossible hand, but I think if she had been less rigid in her stance and had faced down the hardliners then she would have held on to being Prime Minister for longer.

I found her quite buttoned-up, not one for small talk. She was always defensive, giving the impression that she thought everything she said would be used against her. Although in her early visits to Wales she travelled refreshingly lightly, without the control freakery that normally accompanied prime ministerial visits, meetings with her were rarely the genuine discussions they had been with her predecessors. That said, you knew where you stood with her. She didn't say one thing and then do another. With her, it was a case of you said what you had to say and she said what she had to say. There was no dialogue. She did display one common characteristic of successive Conservative leaders, however. They've never recognized that the best way to drive the UK apart is to give the impression that you only listen to governments who either threaten independence or conflict. I told David Cameron and Theresa May more than once that, if you don't show that you're listening to Wales, the only way that the Welsh will respond in order to be listened to is by asking for independence. By making everything a battle, by asking us always to accept and not negotiate, they are constantly poking us in the eye when they could be looking us in the eye instead. This has definitely led to a new grassroots political movement in Wales in favour of greater autonomy, or even independence, that sits outside the Plaid Cyrmu sphere.

While I struggled to find common ground with successive Prime Ministers, I had more fruitful conversations with Nicola Sturgeon, the SNP leader. I think we understood each other and we got on well. We both realized early on that, despite the fact that our party politics were in a different place, we both led governments that could make common cause from time to time. That worked. We were able to sit down as governments and we found plenty of common ground where we could press the UK Government jointly.

This is another example of how the blinkered approach in Westminster acted against their best interests, pushing devolved governments together. We simply couldn't allow Westminster politics to interfere in the relationship between governments in Scotland and Wales. Yes, we met as Heads of Government, once a year in Downing Street, but they weren't particularly constructive meetings. I think, in the early days of each government, we approached it in a spirit of genuine hope of finding negotiated settlements. But when nothing happened, it just descended into an opportunity for us all to rehearse our media lines for the post-meeting interviews. That's a fairly sad indictment of what should be a fundamental building block of UK statecraft, but if anything I'm being charitable. The way governments work with each other is crying out for a better, more meaningful format, ironically along the lines of the joint ministerial meetings in the European Parliament.

The UK needs to change. Its creaking constitution will finally collapse if that change doesn't happen. The UK needs to reflect the fact that it is four different nations. There needs to be more joint decision making. Where there are areas that need joint agreement, then there needs to be a mechanism to allow that to happen. We need greater transparency on funding, because a coach and horses was driven through the Barnett Formula when Northern Ireland got a billion pounds and Scotland and Wales got zilch. (For those who are unaware of the Barnett Formula, it's the formula that determines how funding is distributed around the UK by the UK Government.) That's the sort of action that weakens the ties that bind the UK together.

It was clear to me, though, at the end of 2016, that politics would never again be the same.

SIXTEEN

Uncertain Days and Darkness

BY THE TIME 2017 had arrived, we were still no clearer as to what Brexit meant and how we would shape a UK outside the European Union. Domestically, as a Welsh Government, we passed a few Acts at this time, six in total. But over and above this, it became apparent that we needed to look at how Wales would fare after Brexit, as it was drawing more and more resources away from other areas of government, and critical thinking. This was unavoidable. There was plenty of confusion as to what Brexit actually meant, despite any slogan that stated that 'Brexit means Brexit'. It took a lot of soul-searching from pro-Europeans in Welsh Labour and across the political divide over how best to respond to the referendum result and the policy direction of the May Government. There was a school of thought that we should just come out straight away and say we wanted a second referendum, but politically and morally

I just didn't think that held water at this time, and most of the Cabinet agreed. Our intention as a Welsh Government wasn't to oppose Brexit, but rather to propose how it should work in Wales.

I visited Norway at the start of 2017 as part of my fact-finding mission on a post-Brexit Wales. Norway was not a part of the European Union but it was a member of EFTA, which meant it had favourable access to the Single Market but no control over its operation or rules. Because of the nature of its relationship with the EU, i.e. not part of it but in a trade agreement with it, it was held up as a model of how the UK could be after Brexit.

When I arrived in Oslo, the weather was particularly bad and it was snowing heavily. I fell into the stereotypical British trap of mentioning the weather; I could see that there was heavy traffic going towards the airport and asked the driver if everyone was heading home before the weather got worse. He looked at me quizzically and said, 'No, they're all going away for the weekend.' It wasn't the only difference we found between the British and Norwegian outlook on life.

The politicians I spoke to on that trip were quite clear that they had to passively accept EU rules because that's their biggest market – rule takers not rule makers, as the saying went. The ludicrous argument that Eurosceptics put forward that we were somehow at the whim of European directives with no say and no control was really exposed on a visit to a 'third' country like Norway, but it was never an argument that broke through into the UK media. The Norwegians also explained in painful detail the sheer number of tariffs that exist if you're outside the EU Single Market. I also spoke to Switzerland and Iceland about the same issues and received the same message again and again. Iceland in particular made the point that being such a small country meant they needed as many partners as possible to keep their economy going.

Holding Norway up as a model for post-Brexit Britain wasn't always particularly helpful in any case, as Norway isn't like Britain in one very real way – it has a massive sovereign wealth fund, from North Sea oil. Norway decreed that a certain proportion of their oil wealth was to be put aside. This is why they are one of the few countries in the world without debt. Britain didn't introduce the same safeguards and most of its oil wealth disappeared with the tax cuts in the 1980s.

There were plenty of other conversations going on with our friends and colleagues in Brussels and closer to home, about what a realistic Welsh future might look like for post-Brexit. In the Assembly, where I'd always sought to build consensus when we could, we worked closely with Plaid Cymru in producing a White Paper:

'Securing Wales' Future'. The overriding message from the document was that we needed the least harmful Brexit for Wales. Specifically, that meant staying in the Customs Union and getting the maximum access possible to the Single Market. This statement was a clear case of Wales setting out its stall in a very confusing and uncertain marketplace. I have to say it is a testament to all those involved in producing that White Paper that it has stood the test of time, and even the fiercest critic couldn't put a dent in the content.

There are two footnotes to Securing Wales' Future that are worthy of mention – the first comic, the second tragic. Firstly, at the launch event in London (the only way you can get the interest of UK media is still to go to them, sadly), Neil Hamilton turned up professing to have journalistic credentials and demanding that he be allowed in to question both Leanne Wood and myself. We let him in, and he spent five minutes annoying everyone before being shushed by the real journalists present. Secondly, the White Paper owed a huge amount to a very talented Plaid Cymru AM by the name of Steffan Lewis, who never betrayed a confidence and worked intelligently and diligently on behalf of his party and Wales. Steffan sadly died in 2019, aged just thirty-four. He is sorely missed in the Assembly, where he would have had the brightest of careers, I am certain.

With Brexit still dominating everything, we used the Easter break to get away as a family and travelled to Northern Ireland, to see Lisa's family. I was having breakfast one morning with my sister-in-law, when we heard that there was an announcement from Downing Street: they had called a General Election. I was not too happy with that, I must say! Theresa May had decided to go to the country, and that was that.

So, back from holiday and straight into an election campaign. The prospects didn't look good for Labour at all in the early campaigning days. Things weren't going well on the doorstep, the response to Jeremy Corbyn was poor, particularly from previous Labour voters, and the polls reflected that. I was coming under serious pressure, from Labour MPs in particular, to distance Welsh Labour from Corbyn and to take hold of the campaign, root and branch, in Wales. While I was absolutely committed to leading Welsh Labour in any campaign, it was a daunting prospect coming so soon after our own election, the referendum and the Brexit fallout. I went up to London for a Clause 5 meeting, which is where our manifesto is discussed. It was one of those strange meetings which sums up politics sometimes, in the sense that it was one long, endless argument, but it led to a succinct, five-point manifesto that proved to be very popular.

In those early weeks of the campaign, things were looking bleak right across the country. However, within Wales, we knew that people could respond to Welsh Labour differently. We had already enjoyed a success-ful campaign, against the odds, in 2016, and there was definitely a feeling that we were in a stronger position in Wales than in the UK as a whole. People warmed to the Welsh Labour message and brand in a way that they wouldn't necessarily to UK Labour. So we relentlessly used that to our campaigning advantage. That caused some occasional tension between Welsh Labour and the UK party, and the more avid Corbyn supporters in Wales. This reached its peak when the *Western Mail* ran a front-page story with the headline: 'Carwyn Bans Corbyn from Wales'. This wasn't true, but his planned visit did need to be rearranged in the heat of yet another Ken Livingstone gaffe that occupied the leader's office.

The truth is that we only forged our own path insomuch as Welsh Labour was already a distinct and established entity. People knew who I was, and what I stood for – and some people responded positively to that, just as some others responded positively to Corbyn and his radical agenda. There wasn't, and never has been, a single argument between me and Jeremy. Not person-ally, or through our proxies. We never fell out or argued.

We just did what all teams do, we played to different strengths at different times.

I appeared at many hustings during the campaign, but will always remember the one I did in Penarth. As I came off the stage, at the end of the evening, I thought that it had gone fairly well. Huw Price, my Media Special Adviser, was waiting for me, and he looked ashen. I began to worry immediately. Did I make a huge blunder that I wasn't aware of? He called me into an adjoining room and closed the door. Then he told me what had happened. Rhodri Morgan had died. He'd suffered a heart attack, out on the country roads somewhere, while cycling with his grandson. We were all devastated. Personally, I had lost someone who had been a huge influence on me, a father in politics, without a doubt. I miss him to this day. The campaign had to go on, of course, knowing that Rhodri was no longer with us, but then knowing that we needed to carry on the work that Rhodri had contributed to so significantly. There was a lot of talk at the campaign's conclusion that Rhodri would have enjoyed a hearty laugh at the way the Tory campaign unravelled in the latter stages.

I was campaigning in North Wales at the same time that Theresa May started to get into a little difficulty about social care during the Tory manifesto launch in Wrexham. Up to that point it had been difficult to get anything to stick with Theresa May. She was 'strong and stable' and her party was confident. That confidence filtered through to the Welsh Conservatives, who had launched their campaign in my constituency. There was even talk of Andrew R. T. Davies, the Welsh Conservative leader, standing as the Tory candidate. But both in Wales and the UK, the Tories had taken their poll lead for granted – they overreached in the Welsh campaign, and took too many risks in their manifesto, most especially on the issue that was to be dubbed the 'dementia tax'. That gave us the opportunity to push back.

Allied to the Tory missteps, Jeremy Corbyn stepped up to the plate in the second half of the campaign. He campaigned hard and travelled extensively, going around addressing people old-style, which proved very effective. He had a particular appeal to young people, which I had not seen before. I started to pick up this positive response from young voters in different circumstances. My daughter Seren, for example, came home from college one day to say that they had been discussing the election there and all the students in the discussion said they were going to vote Labour. I had the same message whenever I came into contact with the same age group. A visit to the corner shop near my home led to a conversation about some young people who'd been in talking about the election on their Facebook pages. For the first time, young people were encouraging each other to vote Labour. Now what seemed to be happening was the coming together of the popular Welsh Labour appeal and the Corbyn effect on young people.

On election day, I went to my polling station about 10.30 in the morning. It was busier than it would normally be at that time. Another call into the shop nearby led to the owner telling me that a lot of young people had been in throughout the morning asking where the polling station was. I went to Cardiff that night, to the Labour Party Headquarters, to watch the results coming in. I was there as they were announcing the exit polls. Up flashed the caption 'Conservatives the largest party'. We all did a double-take. Largest party? Not the convincing majority that had been expected? As we took all this in, I looked below the TV screen we were watching, and there, on the wall, was a framed photograph of Rhodri Morgan, smiling broadly. As if he knew.

His smile would have broadened as the night progressed. We won Canterbury. We nearly won Arfon. This had been a largely defensive election for us – the polls at the start were talking about us losing ten seats to the Tories in Wales. There were a number of seats that we hadn't expected to hold, and seats we certainly hadn't expected to win. We won Cardiff North comfortably without the usual level of resourcing for such a key seat.

The same story was repeated up and down the country. The result, of course, left Theresa May without a working majority, and she had to ask Northern Ireland's Democratic Unionist Party (DUP) for their support in forming a government.

Labour hadn't won the election, but there was a tangible euphoria in the party. We had put a halt to the expected 100-seat majority for the Conservatives. How did we manage to do so? I think there were three factors. The young people's vote was one, without a doubt. Then there was the manifesto that Labour produced, which was a fairly left-wing one but people had warmed to it. What I was hearing was that people wanted the state to play a more beneficial role in their lives; people want to know that their government cares about them. The third reason was Jeremy Corbyn, whose work rate during the campaign was exceptional. He was unpopular at the beginning of the campaign, but he turned that around completely. I also think that many Leave supporters voted for us because they felt cast aside, that no one was listening to them.

Our fears in Wales that a large Conservative majority would lead to us being marginalized and ridden roughshod over didn't materialize. The issue we were left to face, however, was what would happen to those devolved issues that would be returned by the European

Union after Brexit. Where would they go? The original proposal was that all powers returning from Brussels would go to London, with the UK Government deciding when, and if, those powers in devolved areas would transfer to the devolved governments. In effect, this meant that England could do whatever it wanted with the returning powers but Wales and Scotland couldn't.

After the election, the new parliamentary arithmetic kicked in and the UK Government realized that it was no longer able to get its own way. David Lidington was put in charge of the Brexit negotiations with the devolved governments. That was a good move. He was far more aware of what was going on than some of his predecessors, and far more of a listener as well. We succeeded in brokering a deal that meant that most of the returning powers would come straight to us. There were some that would be held in suspense, but for everybody. It makes sense for there to be a common set of rules for agriculture and fisheries, for example, but it's important that any decisions on those rules should be agreed by all governments, not just one. It means that England, Wales and Scotland are on a par. The Scottish Government came close to agreeing as well, but eventually decided not to. We had to disagree on that. I just think it was too difficult for the SNP to be seen as agreeing a compromise with the UK Government. Yes, it means we can't exercise every power, but nor can anyone else. Those powers held in suspense can only be used with the agreement of all.

Money was an issue for the devolved governments as well, not just power. As part of the deal to gain the support of the DUP, the UK Government gave Northern Ireland a billion pounds, mainly to be spent on health and education. There should have been a proportional amount given to Wales and Scotland as well. Neither country received a penny. This was a bribe – a bung, pure and simple – and that's exactly what I called it in the pages of *The Times*. As well as the public outcry, we registered formal complaints about it through the correct channels of the Joint Ministerial Council. The UK Government response was that they didn't think there was anything to complain about, and in the utterly perverse constitutional universe that is modern Britain, it is the UK Government that rules over these disputes, and so that was the end of that. Unbelievable. This demonstrated an attitude all too common in these discussions. They quite often seem to fail to grasp the fact that, in many areas, they are only the *English* Government, not the UK Government. They don't legislate for the whole of the UK in so many key areas. As a result, any decision in these areas has to be reached through discussion with the other governments, not through Westminster telling us what to do. There didn't seem to be a full comprehension of this principle. It was unfortunate that the Welsh Conservatives stayed silent about it. They should have demanded the same fairness for Wales.

MOST OF 2017 was taken up with trying to get to grips with Brexit, so it was with great pleasure that we went on a family holiday to Lanzarote that year. Holidays had always had the effect of refreshing me and I went back to work after them raring to go again. But not this time. While on holiday, a new work-related issue cropped up every day. Nothing too major, but there was always something to be sorted. I didn't get a clear day without any work. When I got home, I was as tired as I was when we went. This started me thinking. My original intention was to step down as First Minister in 2019, after ten years at the helm, but was the way I was feeling after the holiday an indication that I needed to reconsider? I decided that staying until 2019, just to round up the ten years, was purely doing so for my own vanity. The reality was that I was finding things that had been relatively straightforward to do in the past a lot more difficult. I began to tire of the endless flow of paperwork and the inability to get away from the job, which hadn't troubled me at all at the start. That wasn't fair on me, my family or my work. So, in September, I decided that I would step down in 2018, not 2019. I had always known that I could never be a politician whose whole life was just politics and nothing else.

I had originally decided to reshuffle the Cabinet in 2018. But now that I was to step down as First Minister that year, I needed to bring the reshuffle forward to 2017. Primarily, this was in order to put people in place who could be in the new government after I'd left, including some who might stand a chance to be candidates for the leadership itself. I decided to do the reshuffle in the week after the half-term holidays.

I had one specific appointment in mind a long time before the reshuffle, albeit not one that would potentially be a candidate for the First Minister post. In 2016, Lord Dafydd Elis-Thomas, former MP and Assembly Presiding Officer, had left Plaid Cymru to become an Independent. We had discussions at that point about him coming into the Government, but the timing wasn't right. I'm not sure it was a huge coincidence that reshuffle rumours increased in intensity in line with the number of conversations I enjoyed with Dafydd, but, even so, I always regarded him as a true statesman, with the sort of political heft, intellect and hinterland who deserved a shot at government. The reshuffle in 2017 was the right time to bring him in, and the newly created role of Deputy Minister for Sport, Culture and

Tourism seemed a perfect fit. With Lib Dem Kirsty Williams already Minister for Education, I now had two members of the Government who weren't in the Labour Party. I think that was a positive way to do politics. People forget that, although Welsh Labour has formed every government since 1999, we have never enjoyed a majority, and reaching out across the Chamber has always been something I've wanted to do – it was more than just a numbers game for me. I strongly believed in harnessing the talents of all progressives.

This was around the time, however, when I had to deal with a difficult situation with one of my ministers, Carl Sargeant, although no one could have imagined at that time where this situation would lead and the tragic end that ensued. Carl and I had known each other for many years. He had been a long-serving member of the Cabinet and he was a working-class man who repre-sented an area of Wales that often didn't have a voice. I often drew the comparison with John Prescott, and what he gave to the New Labour Governments under Tony Blair. Here was someone with a few rough edges who spoke plainly and had real reach into those com-munities in North-East Wales who often felt adrift from Cardiff Bay. He was a good team member, but if he had one political weakness, it was a lack of self-belief and subsequently a willingness to be influenced by others.

When he was low on confidence, he became more easily influenced, and his work rate could drop – things that happen to many of us in life. I spent a lot of time shoring him up. He was still the chirpy character that I had always known, but needed reassurance from time to time. For example, he had become convinced in 2014 that he would be deselected by his constituency. I spent a lot of time reassuring him that all the stops would be pulled out to prevent that, and, indeed, it didn't happen. The suggestion that I had anything but respect for Carl as a friend and colleague is absolutely groundless.

But there was another side of Carl that surfaced from time to time. Some years before, I received an anonymous letter from a woman in Carl's constituency, making allegations that he had touched her inappropriately. I discussed this with him, telling him that I couldn't make a judgement as to whether the allegations were true or not and that there was nothing I could do about it as the letter was anonymous, but I told him to be careful. Carl never made a secret of his fondness for a drink, and he was certainly the most sociable member of our group, so I was worried that he might trip himself up. I knew that Carl had struggled at times with things at home, because of what would come to be described as a 'life event'. It was clear at one point that he wasn't fully focused on his work and I wanted to find out why.

Following the first discussion about what had happened, this 'life event', we developed an additional bond and we talked about it a number of times, not least because I had experienced something similar. I needn't say what that was, as it would be inappropriate to do so, but we had a common experience that we shared our thoughts on from time to time.

After the election in 2016, and after Carl had been appointed to the Cabinet, I was informed of another incident involving his behaviour towards a woman. This time, I knew who the complainant was. She described an incident involving Carl but didn't want to do anything about it. That was a particularly difficult thing to deal with. There was no official complaint, so I had no official procedure to follow. The complainant only wanted to make me aware of the situation so that I could keep an eye on it. I decided to do just that and I didn't tell Carl about her comments. With hindsight, these incidents shone a light on how difficult it was – and remains – for women to come forward with formal complaints about men. Any men. But particularly men in power. It is a shameful stain on our society and it harms everyone.

Then came October 2017. Further allegations came to the surface, with the difference being that this time they were being discussed in a wider context and outside our party. Specific names were mentioned as well.

I knew immediately that this was serious, and I needed the facts as soon as possible. I asked Matt Greenough, my Chief Special Adviser, to look into what had happened, after he received a call about the incidents.

Two women came forward during that process and made written complaints against Carl. Again, the fear they had about reprisals meant that they would only do so with guarantees of anonymity, and they would only speak to either myself or Matt. It was clear that there was absolutely no faith in the processes established by the Assembly for reporting these matters, and it is clear to me now why that was, and remains the case. It is the women who suffer through these processes, not the men. I thought it right at this time to go back to the complainant of June 2016 to see if she wanted to pursue her complaint, given that others had come forward, and it was clear that a pattern of behaviour had now emerged.

With written statements submitted, I knew that I now had to take action. There was no way I could just 'keep an eye on things'. Carl wasn't just a Labour AM, he wasn't just a member of the Government, he was our Equalities Minister. Carl had to be removed from the Cabinet and suspended from the party while an investigation into the allegations was held. In our case, that investigation is done by the Labour Party in London, as that's where the relevant unit is based. I let the party know a few days beforehand so that they knew it was coming, but that's as far as it went. We checked that procedures were right. Very few people knew about it and that's the way I wanted it. Subsequently, some people have asked why I didn't follow the example of what happened with Damian Green and just suspend Carl from Cabinet while a government investigation took place. This is a red herring. Green's case was handled that way for political expediency, and it was a different set of circumstances. I had absolutely no focus on political expediency, just on doing the right thing. The right thing for the women who came forward and the right thing by government. It tells its own story that not one person inside or outside of government questioned the way I handled the reshuffle, or Carl's part in that, until after his tragic death – that includes his colleagues and former colleagues, all of whom told me I had done the right thing in difficult circumstances. Being a leader means you get handed some of the most unpalatable decisions imaginable, and I wouldn't have wished this one on anyone else.

Reshuffles usually take place on a Thursday, and during recess, when it is quiet. But I delayed this one to the Friday of the week after half term because I knew that Carl was in America and wouldn't be back in time.

Given the nature of the conversation I needed to have with him, I wanted to do it face to face. I felt that was the right thing to do. On the Friday, I told everyone involved what the reshuffle was.

There have been allegations that the intention to dismiss Carl had been leaked beforehand. It's nonsense, although in Westminster that's exactly what would have happened. All the most senior journalists in Wales I have spoken to say that they did not know about the reshuffle ahead of time. If they did, then why wasn't anything done with that supposed leaked information? If we wanted to gain some sort of political advantage, we would have made sure it was leading the news, with a helpful spin – setting me up as taking 'tough action'. Again, this is exactly what would have happened in Westminster, and exactly what didn't happen here. The idea of a leak is a nonsense and I think people know it is a nonsense. We were tight-lipped; without question it was the quietest reshuffle we'd done. We didn't want to invite questions about Carl before he and the party had time to get their ducks in a row. I was explicit about that. No journalist was even aware beforehand that there was to be a reshuffle that Friday. There was no leak.

Most ministers stayed in their roles. Alun Davies was reinstated into the Cabinet and made Minister for Local Government and Public Services, replacing Carl.

Although I'd asked Alun to leave government in the past, there was no bad feeling on my part, though I know he didn't take it well at the time. I always thought he was an excellent communicator, and someone willing to offer a considered view at the Cabinet table. Jane Hutt left the Cabinet after being in it from the very start in 1999. It was often said that she was the longest serving minister anywhere in Europe. Her contribution was considerable, and her ability to work across party boundaries was a lesson to all of us. She certainly did nothing out of place to warrant being removed from the Cabinet; I just felt that it was time for a fresh approach.

Jeremy Miles came in as Counsel General, replacing Mick Antoniw, who again did nothing wrong and probably had most reason to feel aggrieved at losing his post. Although he was upset, he didn't show it and was very loyal. I owe him my thanks for that. Jeremy was simply someone who I thought was a potential leadership candidate and deserved a crack. Julie James became Leader of the House after impressing as a deputy minister. As far as the Deputies were concerned, Eluned Morgan came in for the first time, with responsibility for lifelong learning and the Welsh language. Huw Irranca-Davies was children and social care, Rebecca Evans was housing and regeneration and Hannah Blythyn was environment. This was a talented team of deputies, all of whom I felt could also have held their own at the Cabinet table.

The time came to speak to Carl and inform him of the decisions taken. He was surprised and asked what the allegations were. I told him that I couldn't elaborate because that would have led to identifying the women concerned. In the light of what has happened since then, including a tabloid campaign to name the victims of sexual harassment, fuelled by a bunch of small-minded men, I was right not to give any more information. I never thought that Carl would have any truck with that kind of behaviour. In the meeting he said that he accepted that I had to do what I was doing. I suggested he speak to his union to get a lawyer and told him that I would pass the case on formally to the party.

We agreed to keep a very low profile on the whole story, or at least the reasons behind Carl's dismissal. I gave him my word that we wouldn't brief against him – and again every journalist in the land can attest to the fact that this did not happen. It obviously would have been made public that he wasn't in the Cabinet any more, but he wasn't the only one who left in that October and we would treat the story as just that, part of the reshuffle. He was aware that the full story would come out at some point, and his local party would be told why he was going to be suspended, but at least this way he had time to prepare for it.

In the course of the reshuffle later in the afternoon, I learned that Carl had sent a tweet out, saying that there had been allegations against him and that he was going to fight them. I could not understand why he had done that. I can only assume that it had been suggested to him that we would brief against him over the weekend, and give the story to the media, so he should get his case out first. I could have understood this course of action if the people advising him didn't know him – or me – but, again, I suspect that is not the case. I just don't understand what they were trying to do, and they also should have known that when I give my word, it counts. We had no intention of briefing against Carl and I had reassured him on that very point. The whole thing then spun out of control. We had to respond now in a way we hadn't intended, to correct information that Carl had put out. It was needless and unleashed an entirely avoidable whirlwind of speculation.

That was a really difficult weekend. I was told that Carl's family had the media loitering outside their house. They were not a political family, and were unused to such intrusion. Rumours started to escalate, with people saying we've heard it's this, we've heard it's that, and so on. It is difficult thing to grade the seriousness of inappropriate sexual behaviour but, needless to say, some of the rumours running wild that weekend were wide of the mark. That led to the decision on the Monday to make a further statement, to try to calm the situation down. I had, as ever, a series of public engagements planned for the week, so we thought it better to sit down with serious journalists from the broadcasters, rather than getting doorstepped by someone random and things getting out of control. The first thing to emphasize quite clearly was that this was not a police matter, as some had suggested. As much as anything, none of this was fair on Carl himself, because so much that was said just wasn't true.

With the #MeToo phenomenon empowering women to come forward, it also seemed important to show that people in power would believe victims of harassment. The number of times it has been suggested that I should have dealt with this situation by having a 'quiet word' with Carl shows just how necessary the #MeToo movement was, and still is today. It was a difficult time, but I thought it was important to show leadership for those countless women out there who were suffering in silence. Things need to change.

The following day, 7 November, I went into work as usual. I remember the date because it's my father's birthday. Much of that morning had already been put aside because I had decided that I would address the Labour staff members, to reassure them that if they had a complaint of any kind they would be taken seriously and the right attention would be given to them. This was totally unrelated to the situation with Carl, and an already planned response to the growing importance of the #MeToo campaign. Halfway through the meeting, Lesley Griffiths came in and beckoned me to the door. She looked upset. She told me that Carl had hanged himself and that the paramedics were dealing with him. I was stunned. I had to go back into the meeting and carry on where I'd left off, but I could barely concentrate. Sometime later, Lesley called me out again and told me that Carl had died. Everyone was shocked and confused. Why had Carl done this? There were a lot of questions in the midst of silence and grief. I was devastated and bewildered by what Carl had done. I still am.

The story escalated very quickly, and in a highly regrettable and political direction. Leighton Andrews came out with all sorts of allegations about leaks and bullying, none of it supported in later months. I was particularly confused by this behavior, because he had congratulated me on the reshuffle the week before and hadn't expressed surprise about Carl leaving the Cabinet, and nor had anyone else, for that matter. I have no idea to this day why he felt the need to take the action he took, a few days after someone had taken his own life. The death had a devastating impact on everyone involved, but no healing could take place in an atmosphere that became highly charged and unnecessarily political. Leighton was to become the only Labour politician who called for me to stand down during this entire period, which I said I wouldn't do, as there were no grounds for doing so. He phoned up some AMs to ask for their backing and he had little support there, but we ended up with a Leak Inquiry and an inquiry by an independent investigator into bullying. Both found that there was no basis for any of the allegations made.

With the media being fed a string of baseless accusations and outright lies by persons who would not identify themselves, we had to threaten libel action on a number of occasions against journalists who were about to publish things that just weren't true. I have to say the Welsh media was generally more stable in their reporting, as they had a clearer understanding of what they were dealing with and the personalities involved. But more such threats were to follow. Throughout all this, Leighton never spoke to me, so he never asked me directly what my position was on any matter relating to this story. People who were once friends and colleagues were using Freedom of Information requests, and speculating through the media, to try to create a version of events that matched their own thoughts. All they needed to do was pick up the phone and ask me. The tragedy was used as an excuse to reignite old battles, to revisit grudges, to drag up unrelated incidents that had happened years ago. Why? It was all very unseemly. And it was very difficult for us as a government to respond. Everything we could say publicly to disprove the mistruths being thrown at us would either deepen the hurt of the Sargeant family or potentially expose the complainants to media scrutiny and the possible loss of their anonymity. We just had to take it – that was difficult. Difficult for friends, family and some colleagues to understand, and at times difficult personally as well. But I had no interest in deepening anyone's hurt, or exposing the complainants.

We felt some of the impact of this story at home. Someone decided to spray-paint some derogatory slogan on the wall in front of the house. Seren was in at the time and saw this being done. She was understandably upset. In response, I contacted somebody close to Carl's family to inform them of what had happened at our home, and asked this person if things could be calmed down, as they had the family's ear. The response was a solicitor's letter accusing me of slander against that individual.

In November, I had a phone call from a *Daily Telegraph* journalist, reading out a list of names to me and asking me to confirm if any of them were the women who'd made complaints against Carl. Naturally, I wouldn't confirm anything to that journalist. But I knew that the women on the list had one thing in common – they were successful and outspoken, and this alone was enough to annoy a certain cadre of political operatives in Cardiff Bay. This was just a vicious, grotesque and misogynist fishing expedition. And it hasn't stopped. In August of 2018, I had a phone call from a journalist on the *Sun*, again reading out a list of women's names. It was the same list as was read to me the previous November. Having failed to get the press to publish names, someone sent the list to Guido Fawkes, the political website and blog that specializes in being provocative.

My biggest fear is that this period has created an atmosphere where women in Wales don't feel confident in making complaints about any inappropriate behaviour. The women who came forward, and unfortunately there were more, will never have their viewpoint heard. Perhaps not even a fear, but a certainty, and it's still happening. Nobody would have been more opposed to such a witch hunt developing than Carl.

This tragedy has been a very dark chapter in Welsh politics in recent years, but it's obviously been worse for Carl's family than for anyone else. In those first weeks people who were close to both me and Carl tried to arrange for me to speak to the family and I regret that this did not happen. I wanted to express my sorrow at Carl's passing and I wish we could have nipped in the bud these awful and unhelpful conspiracy theories that have simply added more confusion and hurt to an awful tragedy. The protracted legal battles might have been unnecessary, had we managed that human connection at an early stage.

This period certainly had an effect on me and plunged me into depression for the first time in my life. The people closest to me at work noticed the change in me, but I felt like I had to be strong for them as well – they were distraught, working all hours, going through the mill, being questioned and shunned by people they considered friends. I felt responsible for them and wanted to protect them. The ministers who were closest to Carl struggled too. I could see the battles they were going through – they were being told I was this and that, and I'd done this and that, and they were grieving. We were all grieving, and we worked hard to keep each other afloat. And so it was more at home that I allowed my own struggles to get on top of me. I ended up on medication, which made me feel worse initially because I felt that I was weak. I had counselling too, which initially I didn't see as of any great value, but as the weeks went on I was proved wrong and the sessions I received were a great help.

There's much more discussion now about male mental health, and rightly so. It's hard for men to recognize it because it affects their perception of their own masculinity. Nothing could be further from the truth. My message to men who are depressed is this: tell someone, talk, seek help. It doesn't make you less of a man.

SEVENTEEN

Last Year as First Minister

THE BEGINNING OF 2018 was difficult. The previous eight years had begun with me knowing that I was First Minister and that I would continue to be so, barring any political catastrophes. But in January 2018, I knew that it was to be my last year at the helm of Welsh politics. As much as that was a conscious decision of my own making, it was still something I needed to get my head around. It was going to be a big change.

Issues in the news don't respect year ends and beginnings, they just carry on regardless. On an international scale, that meant Brexit was to continue dominating everything else in 2018. In Wales, Carl Sargeant's story would also continue to be at the top of the agenda from time to time, in particular when his son Jack was elected to take his father's place as AM. This was a big step for him. I still felt the loss of Carl and not a day went by when I didn't think of him and all that had happened.

But I also knew that, whatever I was feeling, his family felt so much more. Knowing that, and yet knowing I also couldn't speak to them about it, was an impossible sadness to which there has been no answer. Suicide is a shattering experience, so devastating that we cannot expect the pieces ever to be put back together again.

With the Welsh Labour Party Conference looming, it made sense to start formalizing the process of standing down. I had told Jeremy Corbyn that I would stand down in 2018, but I hadn't told him the exact date or when I would be announcing it. At the start of the conference I informed some of the senior officials in the Welsh Labour Party. I told them that I had come to that decision on my return from our family holiday the year before, and I outlined the reasons that led me to such a choice. I did not mention, however, all I had been through in November 2017, which more than consolidated the decision I had taken previously.

In November 2017 I had found myself in a very low place. This is a difficult experience to talk about. Any version of what I went through at that time could well be misconstrued by some as turning attention towards myself and away from Carl. Nothing could be further from the truth. The black clouds that loomed for me at the end of 2017 led to a severe episode of depression. It was the cumulative effect of the public unfolding of

Carl's story on me personally. I did not feel any guilt for any seemingly wrong decision I had taken, because I genuinely believe that I did the right thing, for the right reasons, and in the right way. Even now I have to balance out the sorrow I feel for Carl's family's loss with the anger and protective feelings I have on behalf of the women who did the right thing by speaking out. It was an impossible conundrum. And with grief and misunderstanding come anger and hurt. In that volatile atmosphere there was little room for the nuance and understanding that such a complicated human and political story required. It took a huge toll.

The doctor diagnosed me with depression and prescribed antidepressants. I'd had short bouts of depression during the course of my life but had always shaken it off. Medication was not a path I wanted to go down. But it was one of two paths that could work for me at the time. The other was counselling, which I preferred.

The way I felt at the time was completely split in two. Outwardly, including at work, I was trying to act completely as usual. No one in the Assembly had any idea that I was near depression, even though they could see I had changed. My work carried on. It's amazing how you can hide these things so that nobody knows except those close to you. But once I was in through the front door of my home, I was a different person.

I would sit in the living room, in the dark, on my own. I remember, one Sunday night in November 2017, I went for a drive with the children to Porthcawl. Once we got there and parked the car, I walked straight to the sea. I didn't take my phone with me. The kids didn't know where I was. I stood there looking at the night sky and the lighthouses in the Bristol Channel. I didn't care about anything in life. I won't go so far as to say that I wanted to end it all, because I didn't; I was just numb to everything, including life itself. Having been standing near the sea for quite a while, my son eventually found me. I knew at that stage that what I was experiencing was really serious.

It was impossible to talk about this situation publicly. I felt very strongly – perhaps wrongly – that nobody wanted to hear that their First Minister was depressed and needed antidepressants to get through the day. And given the debate that Carl's death had started about mental health, it would have seemed somehow inappropriate for me to flag that I was struggling too. So it all had to stay inside. The family dealt with it, and with me, remarkably well. Lisa was so supportive and understanding, Seren and Ruairí too. My father did his best to understand. He said to me at one point that he wished he could help me in a different way, but that he didn't know how because he hadn't dealt with depression before. He helped me in the only way he could, by being there and listening.

When I stood up to make that final conference speech as leader, it wasn't these thoughts and feelings that I talked about, but I stood up to say that I was stepping down as First Minister. When I uttered those exact words, there was an audible intake of breath in the auditorium, because it was so unexpected. Whether it was right or wrong to keep all that inside for so long, it was with a sense of hard-headed pride that I felt like I'd tried and mostly succeeded to right the ships of the Welsh Government and Welsh Labour Party before announcing I was going. The warm reception and standing ovation really touched me, as I know it did Lisa and the kids. As soon as I uttered the words, I felt a huge sense of relief. A weight had been lifted from my shoulders.

That feeling was still there when I sat with my team, Huw Price, Matt, and Jane Runeckles in the Cottage Loaf in Llandudno for a well-earned drink. Jane had been extraordinarily strong during the worst times and was hugely important in carrying us all through. I think we all felt about two stone lighter. We had all carried this decision in private for months, and we'd all carried a lot of hurt as well. As conference delegates filtered from the hall to the pubs of Llandudno, there were lots of hugs and handshakes, shock and surprise. One bloke in the pub – not a politico, it's fair to say – came over to the table to say what a good job I was doing, and he looked pretty confused when I said I'd just announced I was going. But I knew that I had made the right decision. I had no regrets about being First Minister, and I had thoroughly enjoyed my time in office, but I knew that I wouldn't want to go back to it.

I have to say that the support that I had during that conference made me proud and humbled to be part of the Labour family. As with all families, you sometimes don't realize how much love and support there is for you until you ask for help, or say goodbye. Jeremy Corbyn was at the conference on the Sunday. In the middle of his speech, he walked across the stage and shook my hand, having thanked me publicly for my service. That meant so much to me. And it still does.

So the race began to appoint my successor. To be honest, that was the main focus of political activity for those next few months, as it was a fairly quiet summer. I knew that Mark Drakeford wanted to stand and I expected Vaughan Gething to go for it as well. I also knew that Eluned Morgan wanted to stand, but that she was struggling to get enough support from the Labour Group to get nominated. Traditionally, the outgoing First Minister doesn't nominate one of the candidates to be his successor. But, equally, I did think that it would look very odd for us as a party if we had an all-male leadership contest. At first I just made this feeling known publicly, and hoped that one of the Labour Group supporting Mark might lend Eluned a vote to get her on the ballot paper. This didn't happen, which I found a little frustrating and confusing, given the Assembly group's traditionally strong support for closing the gender gap in politics.

I used my final UK Labour Conference speech in Liverpool to announce that I would lend Eluned my nomination to ensure that she got into the contest. This was not tokenism on my part, I just really believed that a woman should be a leadership candidate. One of my last meaningful interventions as First Minister was pushing through a comprehensive Gender Review, which among other things committed us to the idea of Wales becoming a truly feminist country. This is an agenda I feel passionately about, not least having witnessed the attacks on victims of sexual harassment in politics in recent years. I couldn't really square pushing hard on this agenda with withholding my nomination for form's sake, and seeing Eluned miss out as a consequence. I think it was the right decision, and I think the contest was better for it. Despite the fact that I think Mark Drakeford missed a trick by not lending a vote himself, he comfortably won the contest on 6 December 2018. He received 46.9% of the vote in the first round of the contest, and 53.9% in the second round against Vaughan Gething.

Declaring my decision to step down didn't mean that my health improved immediately. Lisa and I, along with some friends, went away for the October half term to Newport, Pembrokeshire. We enjoyed the food and the walks in this beautiful part of Wales. However, completely out of the blue, on the second evening, without any warning, I had a severe headache. Lisa was in the shower and I was in the bedroom getting ready to go out for dinner when it happened. That's the last thing I remember. Lisa came out of the shower to see me standing there asking, 'Where am I? What have I done today?' She told me that we were in Pembrokeshire and I asked her why we were there. She asked me if I felt any numbness down one side. I said no. She asked me who the Prime Minister was. I said Theresa May. I then looked in the mirror and asked, 'How have I got a beard?' (I'd grown a beard that autumn.) Lisa was, by then, sufficiently alarmed.

She told our friends that we were going home. I discovered later that we stopped in Pont Abraham services on the way back, but I have no memory of that. There was a period of just over two hours when I didn't know what had been going on. But by the time I was home, I had come round again. So we decided against going to

A&E. The following day we thought it best to ring the out-of-hours service. When I described the symptoms to them, they asked if anyone in my family had had a stroke. I said that my father and both my grandfathers had. Anyone in your family had a brain haemorrhage? Yes, I said, my auntie. She had a fatal haemorrhage when she was fifty-one. That was enough to keep me in for some tests, and that was the first time in my life that I had to stay in hospital overnight.

I had a CT scan. It was clear. That was good, or so I thought. They said that such a scan didn't always pick up everything, so I needed one more test – a lumbar puncture. That was not straightforward at all. They couldn't get the needle in. So they had to try larger and larger needles. In the end, I just said that I didn't care what size the needle was as long as it didn't have a picture of a horse on the packet! All this was done with a local anaesthetic, which wasn't exactly 100% effective. As they were doing this, one of the nurses said that I had been to the same school as his mother. I asked her name but did not recognize it when he said it. I then asked when she was born. He replied 1948! That helped my spirits. With the right needle finally applied, I stood up and two anaesthetists asked me, 'Can we have a selfie with you?' Ever the politician, and even in my pyjamas, I couldn't refuse.

They eventually found a lesion in the front of the brain that had affected my short-term memory. That made sense, as I was experiencing loss of memory for details I would otherwise have no problem with. I would forget names, for example. There was one occasion, during Black History Month, when I was making a speech in the Welsh College of Music and Drama: I lost all sense of why I was there. I froze for a few seconds before recovering my place and remembering what I was doing. It was a strange experience. Thankfully, this never happened in the Assembly Chamber. The doctors have told me that it was an isolated incident and unlikely to repeat itself.

December 2018 arrived, and my family were once again in the Assembly with me, this time to see me stand down as First Minister. I have to say that I was very emotional that day. I was very touched at the ovation I received from my fellow AMs. We had been through a lot over those nine years, and what came across from the opposition benches was that, while we obviously had strong disagreements on points of policy, they recognized I was a passionate champion for Wales and the institution. I was very moved by the messages of support and congratulations I received, and the farewell event in the Assembly after the end of formal business was a real honour. I know that one person from my office, Jo Hunt, made it her life's mission to make that evening a success, and she pulled it off with some style. But despite the meticulous preparation on my behalf, I had another episode during my farewell speech. I really wanted to thank all my team, one by one, for their work and support. I went through them all, but I completely forgot one: Beth Davies. I forgot to mention her and then, when I remembered that I should, I gave her the incorrect name. I have apologized to her a thousand times since. That was the last remnant of the episode that happened in October. It hasn't happened since.

When January 2019 arrived, I was once more a back bencher, for the first time since 2000. It was a big change. That change hit me one particular Tuesday. Normally the busiest, most stressful day of the week, as I prepared for Cabinet, the Labour Group meeting and First Minister's Questions. My every movement timed to within seconds. And now here I was in my Assembly Member's office, and we had run out of tea bags. What shall we do now? I asked myself. Then it dawned on me. I could simply walk out of the office, on my own, and buy a pack of tea bags myself. That hadn't been possible for years.

EIGHTEEN

Regrets and Prime Ministers

WHAT HAVE I regretted in politics? My main regret is that I didn't succeed in reorganizing local government. I believe that's something that needs doing urgently. Having twenty-two local authorities in a nation as small as ours means that we simply waste too much time, energy and resources. I know that there are those inside local government who perceive this as some sort of attack, and the fact we've never managed to get this done is owed at least partially to the fact that we've never broken down that assumption. But I used to be a councillor; I understand the pressures. I always just wanted – and still want – to put local government on a far more secure footing for the future. Some of our councils are too small to be viable and they are totally reliant on having exceptional people doing more hours than they should – that's unsustainable. I would have been happy to give local authorities more powers, as long as they were able to exercise those powers responsibly. This is something that will have to happen in the future.

I was never the most tribal of politicians, which while it always raises a few eyebrows in your own party, I think it is a trait that all good leaders share. You have to see the other point of view. And I enjoyed working across party boundaries and bringing talented people like Kirsty Williams and Dafydd Elis-Thomas into government. You see the value of being slightly less partisan even more when you step away from the frontline. I'm much more reflective in terms of what I say in the Assembly now. I obviously maintain a deep interest in politics, but I can't see myself taking part in any elected form of politics again. I'd be lying if I said something didn't spark inside me when people ask me to run for this or that – I do have a naturally competitive instinct, challenging myself as much as anything – but it is nothing more than a spark at the moment.

I shall stand down as Assembly Member for Bridgend in April 2021, which means that I will have served my constituency for twenty-two years. It has been a tremendous honour for me to represent my home area as its first Assembly Member in my country's first Parliament. And it goes without saying that it was then a massive honour to be First Minister for nine years. But

I must say that I am thankful that this leg of the journey is done, even though it has been immensely challenging and rewarding.

I sometimes get asked if I'd return to law, but I definitely won't be going back into legal practice. I've been away from it for far too long. It was a fantastic honour, though, to be appointed a law professor at Aberystwyth, and I'm looking forward to getting my teeth into the academic side of law again. If there are areas outside of politics that appeal they would be broadcasting, business consulting and sport administration. I've been lucky enough to be involved in some of this work already.

It won't come as a surprise to anyone who knows or shares my love of trivia to read that I was absolutely gutted to be dropped from a planned appearance on *Celebrity Mastermind*. I had been accepted and had chosen the charity that was to receive any money I won. But then I received a message to say that there had been a mix-up, and my place was filled by Shaun Ryder of Happy Mondays fame! I was absolutely certain that I would have nailed my specialist subject – Welsh rugby in the 1970s – but, on reflection, this may well have put the producers off. Having had to slog through a lot of difficult engagements, I had really been looking forward to the show, and my poor office staff had to draw lots to decide who was going to tell me it had been pulled.

I WORKED WITH four UK Prime Ministers over the years. Tony Blair was in office when I was a minister, not First Minister. He was someone who could hold a crowd fantastically well. If you were in an auditorium where he was speaking, you would be convinced that he was talking to you. He was, and remains, a phenomenon in terms of his ability to communicate a message – and there's no question he was the right leader at the right time for Labour. Whatever your thoughts about the Iraq War, it is wrong to dismiss his place in Labour history and some of the language used about him by fringe elements inside the Labour movement today is absolutely shocking. Tony's voice and speaking style have been so often mimicked that when I once received a supportive call from him, I was convinced it was a put-up job and not really him at all – I was ridiculously guarded in everything I said on that call. After a few texts and checks I found out it was him after all and called back full of apologies!

The best speaker I ever saw, incidentally, was Bill Clinton. He addressed the Labour Party Conference in Blackpool in 2000. He was astonishing. He had a chatty, folksy style and you would swear that it was just you and him in the room. He has quite a gift.

Gordon Brown was Prime Minister for three months after I became First Minister. He is a very committed and principled man, and I've enjoyed getting to know him more in the years since his untimely election defeat. It's very sad that he didn't have more time as Prime Minister and, with every year that passes, it becomes more and more clear that the decisions he took after the 2008 crash were absolutely spot on. He pulled the UK out of what would have been a crippling depression. He did that, along with Alistair Darling. History deserves to be kind to them both, and it is a shame that neither of their personalities were allowed sufficient time to come through in a way they deserved.

Then came David Cameron. Our first meeting gave rise to quite a funny story. When we had finished our meeting, we both stood up. We are of very similar height and as we stood next to each other we were both apparently doing something that caused our staff some merriment. One of my team told me afterwards that we were both like two meerkats, trying to make ourselves taller than the other. They were all suitably amused but we had no idea that we were doing it!

That same day, he was seated on a settee which was positioned in front of a window. He asked me how the economy was going in Wales. Outside the window behind him there was a large crane on a building site. It had been idle for a very long time but had started moving again the week before Cameron's visit. I started my answer to his question by saying that things were beginning to improve and went on to say, 'That crane over there started moving last week for the first time in a while.' Normally, I would expect people to turn round and look at what I was pointing at. But he didn't. He just carried on staring at me. I couldn't help thinking that stemmed from quite a strange and practised style of personal engagement, where you'd never shift your gaze from someone, no matter how unnatural it might feel.

He was quite the operator, Cameron. I could have a decent enough conversation with him and then his media people would put out something wildly different in tone and content. I know many people assume that's how politics works at all times, but, actually, in leader-to-leader conversations, you normally observe a certain protocol. Not when it came to Mr Cameron, I found. He is also far posher than he likes to let on. And full of confidence to the point of overconfidence. I think that's what we saw with the Brexit referendum. He got ahead of himself after the successful Scottish referendum, which, let's face it, owed little to the Tory Party, and subsequently tried to take too much on himself, thinking he could get what he wanted. He was supportive enough of devolution, but he certainly used the different colours of government in Wales and Westminster as a political weapon when he came under pressure. The attacks he licensed on the Welsh NHS were particularly over the top – calling Offa's Dyke the line between life and death. A comment that I think did more damage to the Tories in Wales than it ever did to us, but one that still angers NHS staff here to this day – and you can see why.

Finally, there was Theresa May. Whereas, with Gordon Brown, you got to see past his public persona pretty quickly, I can't say that ever happened with her. She had her prepared lines and never strayed from them. Small talk was not in the script, although I did once glimpse through the Robocop armour in our final meeting in Westminster. She had been on the receiving end of a humiliating defeat in the Commons regarding her Brexit deal, and it seemed as though the writing was on the wall for her premiership. We met in Westminster Palace rather than Downing Street, which has a tiny private office. There were bottles of Christmas whisky lined up on the table behind, waiting for signatures. It was a little sign of humanity and vulnerability, and her demeanour that day was slightly more open. Others have said to me that in reality she isn't like that, and I suspect that she felt that she had to perform in a certain way as Prime Minister.

With Lisa being from Northern Ireland, I had more than a political interest in that country. I am always impressed as to how Peter Robinson and Martin McGuinness got on with each other and worked together. Peter was First Minister of Northern Ireland from 2008 until 2016, serving the Democratic Unionist Party. Martin was with the Republican Sinn Féin and was Peter's Deputy First Minister. On Peter's retirement, he stated in more than one interview that the two had never fallen out and had never stopped speaking to each other, even when they strongly disagreed. 'We still held each other's confidence; if those issues go public before an agreement can be reached both sides are damaged,' he said. 'The ability to keep confidence is a big loss in the current time. There have been a lot of "he said, she said" issues which have damaged the confidence the parties have in each other.' Today, there's a lot of that in politics generally. It's great to see that Northern Ireland now has a functioning government again.

One leader with whom I have worked very closely is Jeremy Corbyn. We get along very well personally. When he was elected he was untried, untested and very much of the Left, of course. We were all wondering how it was going to work out. My politics weren't his politics, that was evident. It was pretty clear that he had a brand – Corbynism; whereas I was a pragmatic Labour leader, always aware of my values, but always conscious of the need to get things done. There were issues over the years that we disagreed about, but that has never influenced the way that we got on. I hope that's something that future Labour leaders in Westminster can reflect on. Politicians like Ed Milliband, who were unquestionably closer to me politically, found almost weekly ways to rub me and the Welsh Labour Party up the wrong way, through a basic lack of thinking and respect for devolution.

And so it was somewhat unlikely that Jeremy and I found so much common cause but, as often in life and politics, it owed more to mutual respect than to a completely shared vision of the world. He's certainly not the dour Leftie that people try to make out he is, and he had a very 'good war' in 2017, taking on Theresa May and outperforming all expectations. But it looked like 2019 was an election too far for him – perhaps. For those around him – certainly. A vindictive, purist form of politics was allowed to fester inside the party at a UK level, which resulted in the disastrous defeat against a Boris Johnson-led Tory Party. Our failure to tackle anti-Semitism inside the party, and our very public flip-flopping over Brexit, was showcasing to the voting public everything that was wrong with politics. I normally asked a surrogate to attend Labour NEC meetings on my behalf, but I made sure I was there for the one where we voted on adopting the IHRA definition of anti-Semitism. It was something we had already done as a Welsh Labour Government, without hesitation. And so I was deeply troubled by some of the remarks I heard around that time, and I remain deeply concerned about our need to win back the trust of Jewish people in this country.

IF THERE HAS been a heavy focus on international events and, indeed, sport in this book and my time as First Minister, I make no apology for it. Just as Rhodri Morgan saw his role as leader to let devolution settle and succeed in the minds of the people of Wales, so I saw it as my role to use that springboard and start selling Wales to the world. The expansion of the international offices; the purchase of Cardiff Airport; chucking the kitchen sink at NATO, the Ryder Cup and attracting the Champions League Final – these are all pieces of the jigsaw that are starting to form a picture of Wales in the world's eyes. In diplomacy terms, people talk about the importance of 'soft power' – how your wider cultural offering as a country can open doors – and for me sport has always had a fundamental role to play here.

I'm not going to pretend that, for a sports nut like me, it isn't also a lot of fun to see Wales succeed first hand on so many occasions. But I'll never deny that, for the vast majority of people who think about Wales, it is our sporting and cultural stars that represent the nation – not the First Minister or the Cabinet.

Wales' presence on the world rugby stage is long established. And we have consistently contributed to the development of the game, achieved significant successes and produced genuine world stars. In rugby, Wales has existed as a nation for a long, long time. To be able to share in significant successes for the Welsh national team as First Minister has been a huge bonus. During my period in office, Wales has won two Grand Slams. In other words it has beaten all the other teams in the same annual Six Nations contest: England, Scotland, Ireland, France and Italy. That this success has an impact on the public mood and national sentiment is beyond question.

I was fortunate enough to meet Warren Gatland, at that time the Welsh national team's head coach. He is an unassuming New Zealander who has contributed a great deal to Wales, not only on the rugby pitch.

It has been a rather more unexpected surprise, but no less welcome, to be able to experience the success of the Welsh football team in recent years – most especially at the incredible Euro 2016 Championships. Football has historically played a quieter role in Wales, in terms of national significance at least. More people play the game week in, week out in parks throughout the country, but with few bright moments like the 1958 World Cup aside, rugby has always had the more storied history. But in 2016, it was the turn of the round ball to promote Wales far and wide, not the oval one. Wales did exceptionally well in the European contest that year, reaching the semi-finals. The victories over Russia and Belgium in particular will never be forgotten. And nor will the wonderful behaviour and spirit of the fans who travelled to France, making many new friends for our country. It propelled Wales to new heights in terms of global perception. The reach of football's influence is far wider and deeper than rugby. So when Wales succeeded as they did in the Euros, the word spread further.

I was in a bar in Paris watching that semi-final game. It was a heart-warming and incredible experience to hear people of all nationalities chanting '*Pays de Galles, Pays de Galles!*' After the Euros, if I was talking to people in Paris and they asked me where I came from, I would, as always say Wales. If that was questioned, I would say, 'Wales. Gareth Bale?' 'Ah yes, Gareth Bale!' they would reply, recognizing one of Wales' foremost football stars in the 2016 competition.

There was a time when sport was really the only

standard bearer for Welsh political identity. Now we have our own Parliament, this is no longer true, but that doesn't mean we should limit our support for those who are proud to fly our flag on the global stage.

I'VE NEVER KNOWN a time when there has been so much political turmoil. Two words have dominated the last few years: Brexit and Trump. The US President seems to think that he's living in a reality TV show; for the rest of us it feels more like a fast-paced horror movie. There are right-wingers across the world threatening the stability of their countries and, consequently, the rest of us as well. And Brexit has caused so much uncertainty that we will take a long time to recover from it.

If prosperity is to be evenly spread, it needs certainty, not chaos. We saw that in the late 90s and early 2000s, when people were given more opportunities under New Labour and living standards rose for millions. The idiocy of bankers put an end to that in 2007 and we're still feeling the effect of the damage done. As ever, it was those who were less well-off who were hurt the most by the greed of those at the top. The massive economic upheaval of that period left everyone looking for someone to blame. Sadly, history shows us that the people who take the blame are the weak, the powerless and the vulnerable – those people who in actual fact are much more likely to reap the whirlwind of economic instability.

Our future relationship with the EU is still a huge question mark hanging over the country. I've said for years that Ireland will be the defining issue and I still cannot see how there can be different customs arrangements put in place that do not exacerbate tensions between north and south. Much of the fuel that sparked the Troubles initially isn't there any more. But we should be very mindful of igniting old animosities. Does this now mean that we should consider the issue of Northern Ireland becoming part of the Republic? Perhaps. We now have a generation of Protestants who don't remember the Troubles. They see the South now as a more prosperous, liberal state, which the North is not in the same way. Twenty-five years ago the South would have been seen as backward in terms of its social make-up and economy. No longer. One possible sticking point beyond tribal loyalties is that the South doesn't have a National Health Service while the North, of course, has the NHS.

I've long been of the opinion that a bad Brexit will contain the seeds of the UK's destruction as a nation state. Our constitution is not fit for purpose and it needs urgent change in order for the UK to stay together.

New arrangements are needed that reflect the fact that the UK is not one nation with one government, as it was last century. There are four nations, each with their own government and priorities, but all with the same objective of keeping the same core agenda as a united kingdom. Other countries across the world have managed to do this, but for some reason we don't seem willing to grasp the nettle. Conservatism seems to dominate along with an overly entrenched respect for a tradition that's no longer relevant. Post-imperial attitudes still prevail, driven by a buccaneering spirit that seems to suggest that we once 'ruled the waves' and we still can. A country should be mindful of its past but it shouldn't try to live in it. As soon as countries start harking back to some kind of glorious era, they're on the slide. The reality is that the world doesn't owe the UK a living. The idea that the EU needs the UK more than the other way round is, quite simply, preposterous. We need each other.

That harking back to a previous era is very selective too. Because, if we go back to the 1970s and Britain's story, we see a country that was desperate to join the European Economic Community because our economy was tanking. The Commonwealth countries, there as a direct consequence of the imperialism that many long for, couldn't help us in the same way that the European

Union could. The EU will always hold together. There has been no sign of another member country wanting to break away after the UK decided to do so. That's what Brexiteers had hoped for, the disintegration of the EU following Britain's decision to leave. Other countries would follow Britain's lead, they thought. It hasn't happened and I hope, for the sake of peace and stability on our continent, that it doesn't happen.

This was the subject of a head-to-head debate I had with Nigel Farage, in the Millennium Centre in Cardiff. He is a very tricky operator to battle against. His supporters were in the audience in big numbers, making a lot of noise and being generally unpleasant. Farage was always careful in his remarks to make statements you can't refute, because they're based on a wilfully fantastical notion of the future. He'd say things like, 'You can't do that, because German car manufacturers will respond in such and such a way.' Well, you couldn't say they wouldn't, because you didn't know that, no more than he knew they would. He liked to say things like, 'The EU will be desperate to deal with us if we do this and that.' You can only rebut that by giving your best guess about what would be likely to happen, using the evidence you have available. And while that might be the more grown-up approach, it wasn't the most effective way to quieten down Farage and his supporters.

The only time I could get near him was when he said that 77% of our laws are made in the EU. I could reply to that instantly: 'Where do you get that figure from?' 'From a German chancellor,' was the reply. 'Which one?' I asked. No reply. But he is tricky. He says things that are completely off the wall, but in such a way that they sound like common sense.

What he has channelled, as have other leaders in other countries, is a general dissatisfaction among people with the current system. In the UK, there's a growing unease with the traditional two-party system, there's unrest. This has led to the dissatisfied focusing their feelings on parties such as UKIP and the Brexit Party. There is a genuine feeling that 'some' people have done well, but not 'us'. The uneven spread of economic success that has been seen in the UK is the issue for the Labour Party. Too much of it was based on employment that was flexible but actually insecure. It was employment that people felt wasn't worthwhile. People weren't happy with what they saw as an elite, more in London than Cardiff, living a life that most couldn't aspire to. They were right.

I still live in the town in which I was brought up. I go out shopping here, my children went to schools here, I go to the pub, I watch the rugby, I come home. For too many politicians, this is not a living reality. For most voters, it's not the perceived reality. I understand the dissatisfaction this creates for so many individuals. I'm not so sure that this means the end of the two-party system in the UK. We have, after all, heard all this before. The 1980s gave us the SDP, with their aim of challenging the two-party system, regarded then as being tired and broken. The SDP went, however, and the two-party dominance prevailed.

Cutting through each individual political or economic issue, and the merits or otherwise of the two-party system in British politics, is the way that the public perception of politics and politicians has changed. The truth has always been debated in politics, but I rarely saw politicians openly lie. Now some don't even pretend that what they say is actually true, and they get away with it. Consequently, we are in an age where people are likely to accept that politicians will always lie. That is an appalling state to be in.

Throughout my career in government, I've often been asked the question, 'Should I go into politics?' This is usually asked by young people. It's a tough question to answer. Firstly, there are very few jobs that you can lose while being told publicly in front of a cheering crowd! These days, it's far more difficult to get people into politics at all because of the intense scrutiny on social media, scrutiny that far too often turns to abuse.

For me, it's water off a duck's back. But it has turned far more personal, and in some cases, criminal. That's not a good environment for politics. Some of the abuse directed at women in politics in particular has been utterly vile and shaming – it has shone a spotlight on views that many people thought had died out long ago.

So, while it has always been difficult to attract people into politics, the reasons differ with the times. Most people who do make the leap, regardless of party, come into politics to make a difference, as they see it. You might well attack somebody politically, but you should be having a go at what they are saying. Now, the character of the politician is dissected, especially in America. It's the difference between destroying people and destroying their argument.

I have always thought that the people who are best equipped for elected office have done something besides working in politics. If you spend all your time in the political atmosphere, without ever having done anything else, it is difficult to get perspective and a proper handle on the bigger picture. When you've lived and worked a little in the outside world, and you know the time is right, you have more to offer. But I'd recommend that people still do put their names forward and give it a shot. It is up to all of us currently working in politics to do more to tackle the online abuse and other obstacles, so we can attract the brightest and the best from all walks of life.

THE INSTABILITY that has defined the last five years of our politics has meant that the bonds that have tied people to the British state have weakened considerably. This has led to a significant growth in curiosity about independence, particularly in Wales. I wouldn't characterize it as rapidly growing support at this stage, but there is certainly a heightened awareness of what an independent Wales could look like. Many Labour Party members have come up to me in recent months to say that perhaps we shouldn't dismiss independence out of hand. That's something that's definitely changed. I wouldn't have heard that even two or three years ago.

Personally, I don't support independence. I can't see what it gives us, other than challenges which would be difficult to overcome. The arguments are just the same for me as the ones we adopted for staying in the European Union. It won't make me or anyone else more Welsh than we are now to live in a separate state. I do fear that we could become independent by accident if Scotland and Northern Ireland break from the EU and England decides it could happily carry on alone. There is a feeling in certain political circles in England that Wales is an irrelevance – a subsidy junkie that England can do without. And at the end of the day, Brexit is really all about England and what England wants. You can look at the work of Professor Richard Wyn Jones at Cardiff University, who has found that there is a strong correlation between Brexit voting and English identity. It's the Westminsterizing (that'll be in the dictionary in twenty years, believe me) of all that's happened in the UK. I firmly believe, however, that a far stronger Welsh voice is needed within the UK, and a proper constitution as well, not the ramshackle one we have now, which will not last much further into the future.

I must say that I'm not too confident about that future. I'm concerned politically for Wales, not only in terms of talk of independence by accident or otherwise, but also in economic terms. We have done well in terms of bringing investment in, and unemployment was coming down. I worry now that Brexit will undo all of this hard work. In terms of produce, we will always have beef and milk all year round. But we will never have vegetables and fruit all year round. So we will be dependent on other markets. That's why we had rationing in the war, because it wasn't possible to import things. People seem to forget that. Ninety per cent of Welsh fish is exported. So we obviously need the markets for it. Any delays in getting to those markets can be the difference between a lorry full of fish to sell and a lorry full of fish gone off.

I'm particularly worried these days, of course, about the future of my children in this uncertain world. They do have one huge advantage, however, in that they both have Irish passports. That's the best passport you can have, to my mind. Why? Because it gives you freedom to travel and live in the UK but also in the EU as well. That's a great gift that their mother has given them. She has the same passport, of course. Which leaves me in a very peculiar position. My children will be able to live and work freely in twenty-eight countries, but, for me, it'll just be the UK. That's the wall that Brexit has built around us.

NINETEEN

Family Reflections

THIS BOOK STARTED with family and it will end with it. As I've mentioned, I am an only child, and I was an only grandchild on one side of the family. I have two first cousins, Ceri and Emyr, who live 'on the Waun' with their families as well. I don't know if it's true of everyone in that situation, but, in my case, being the 'only one' has brought with it a fear of being alone. I have always wanted a big family because I came from such a small one. And that family has grown smaller and smaller. The only ones I have left now are my father and my Auntie Maureen (my dad's brother's wife) and the cousins. They are very much a part of our lives.

That feeling of perceived isolation has surfaced from time to time over the years. It can mean that you are a bit shy, which I was at the beginning. I suppose, on a more constructive point, it can lead you to make more of an impression on your world. It certainly highlights the importance of family to me. It is enormous. But it's unfortunately true that many politicians focus entirely on politics, and family life becomes secondary. It never was for me. I wouldn't have been able to do what I have done without the support and understanding of my family.

One of the greatest things my family has given me is the Welsh language. Everybody on all sides of my family are Welsh and Welsh-speaking, for as far back as we can go. It was important to me that my children, despite growing up in a largely English-speaking town as I did, would be able to speak the language fluently, and they do.

When I was a child, pretty much everybody in Brynaman spoke Welsh all the time. The colliers spoke it, the District Nurse spoke it. The shopkeepers spoke it. English was seen as a 'posh' language. My father has often told me that you could go for days when he was growing up without hearing English at all.

Sadly, things have changed. Although two-thirds of the village speaks Welsh, you don't often hear it among young people, even though they speak it and are educated in it. The position of the language is still not secure. Growth in the south-east has been balanced by a loss of communities in the west as people move in who can't speak Welsh. Although it has to be said that many of these people are very supportive of the language, they do inevitably change the everyday language of a community, which the education system then tries to address. For me, though, passing the language on to my kids was a fundamental part of keeping a family tradition.

Lisa and I had our twenty-fifth wedding anniversary in December 2019. As you know by now, she has had incredibly bad luck with her health. She didn't deserve such a bad run. But despite all that she's been through, she's always been there for me. We've had some challenging times as a couple, just as I have had in my politics. The support I've had from Lisa has been overwhelming. It is also true to say that, since stepping down as First Minister, I have been given a list of things to do around the house, a list which will no doubt grow much longer once I step down as Assembly Member completely. That could be an interesting time. On the occasions when I do some odd job, if I have to ask my father to borrow a drill, my father has to accompany it, just in case I demolish the house or something. I think he's spent most of his life wondering how his son could be so useless in the subjects he taught.

Seren was particularly supportive of me during the difficult times of the Carl Sargeant story. She's a great listener, quite streetwise and very canny. She often gave me advice well beyond her years. Her sharp wit helped a lot too. There's a lot that I can take from the way I have seen her as someone who's gone from a very difficult place to someone who has blossomed.

Ruairí, as a child, was extremely talkative, then, when his voice broke, he seemed to lose half his vocabulary. We have very similar interests and we do a lot together, such as go on train journeys around Europe. He is reliable and kind-hearted and has shown equal support but in a different way to his sister.

My father has always been my rock. Steady. Always there for me. I can't begin to imagine what it must have been like for him to watch my mother's decline. But he dealt with the situation with dignity. My mother's funeral was on 23 December 2009, a few days before Christmas. My children were nine and seven at the time, and, on Christmas day, my father came to our house and he did his level best to make it as special a Christmas for Ruairí and Seren as he could. I was astonished at how he could spend time with them, play with their presents, almost as if nothing had happened. My respect for him was immense. He has also been fortunate to have met Amy, his companion ('girlfriend' seems like the wrong word), and she has provided him with a lot of support.

I'm not good doing things as a loner. I need someone to talk to, someone to tell what I've done. I've no doubt that, as well as coming from being an only child, this compulsion also goes back to some formative influences of my roots in those three West Wales villages. Whenever we went back there on family visits, when I was a child, we had a definite route that we took from relative's house to relative's house. We kept the same pattern every time we went on our visits. There were so many relatives there that it would be a full day out. But I loved these visits, and relished the opportunity to share my adventures and stories with the family in this part of Wales. If we called at the home of my Great-Uncle Evan in Cwmgors, for example, as we would be leaving, he'd ask in Welsh, 'Chi'n mynd lan?' ('Are you going up?') in reference to going to see my grandmother's sister, Lucy-Ann. As soon as we got to her house, she would ask, 'Chi wedi bod lawr?' 'Have you been down?' That's how it was every time, for years.

In Auntie Lucy's home the fire would be burning in the hearth all year round. There was an old valve radio there, a toilet outside and the bath in the kitchen, with a lid over it. On one of the walls, she'd hung a picture called 'Christ of Galilee'. It was one of those 1970s 3D pictures and, in this one, Christ's arm moved as you changed your position round the room. She thought that this was wonderful. Her son, John, is the last of the five original cousins on that side of the family.

With the passing of all the family in these villages,

there are no more visits, of course, but also no one to share memories with. I have so many photos in so many family albums of these people, and they are treasured. But I'm the last person who knows who all these people in the photos are.

I've always had that fear of being alone. Not being alone in a room. But isolation. It's always been there with me. I think this has driven me to be more of an extrovert, which drove my career path in law and which then drove me into politics.

I have a need to share. That has and does happen in a work environment, of course. But it's in my family that it has always happened best, and where it is still happening, for real. I've had a rewarding time in politics, with some extremely difficult times thrown in. But above all that, I was a human being and a family member, and as important as the political world is, life is not just politics.